Bullying

The Secret to Overcoming Bully Bosses and Crazy Co-workers

(How To Protect Your Children From Being Bullied Or Cyber bullied)

Robert Milne

Published By **Cathy Nedrow**

Robert Milne

Bullying: The Secret to Overcoming Bully Bosses and Crazy Co-workers (How To Protect Your Children From Being Bullied Or Cyber bullied)

ISBN   978-1-9992826-1-5

No part of this guidebook shall be reproduced in any form without permission in writing from the publisher except in the case of brief quotations embodied in critical articles or reviews.

Legal & Disclaimer

The information contained in this book is not designed to replace or take the place of any form of medicine or professional medical advice. The information in this book has been provided for educational & entertainment purposes only.

The information contained in this book has been compiled from sources deemed reliable, and it is accurate to the best of the Author's knowledge; however, the Author cannot guarantee its accuracy and validity and cannot be held liable for any errors or omissions. Changes are periodically made to this book. You must consult your doctor or get professional medical advice before using any of the suggested remedies, techniques, or information in this book.

Table Of Contents

Chapter 1: Empowering Children
Building Self-Confidence and Self-Esteem

Children must increase self-self assurance so one may be empowered and to keep away from turning into the dreams of bullying. Those who revel in assured in themselves are more able to face up to dangerous messages and confront bullying methods. Below, we're able to delve into a few achievable strategies to encourage children's resilience and self-self perception.

Promoting high first-rate self-talk is a enormously powerful manner to enhance their self-self warranty. We can assist them in expertise how their internal communique affects their self-perception and feelings via using education them to understand and combat bad self-communicate. It's crucial to strain the price of self-compassion and remind them to treat themselves well. Encourage them to update horrific, self-deprecating beliefs with ones that validate their charge and ability. They might also additionally say, "I am capable and worth of admire," in choice to, "I'm now not correct enough." We give them the system they need to increase a greater awesome self-photo thru actively encouraging superb self-speak.

One of the most essential steps in boosting a infant's self-self assurance is spotting and applauding their skills and accomplishments. To assist them discover their man or woman capabilities and passions, it's miles crucial to encourage them to pursue quite a number of pursuits and interests. Caretakers can encourage a sense of success and decorate their self guarantee by the use of giving them chances to illustrate their abilties.

It is important to increase venues for youngsters to reveal their artwork once they exhibit capacity in a particular subject, like paintings. This can entail displaying off their works at activities within the community or at home, or it might even entail applauding their creativity in the the front of the family. Caregivers can assemble a experience of pleasure and make stronger the idea that their present is profitable and deserving of acknowledgment with the useful resource of recognizing and appreciating their modern skills.

It's essential to maintain in mind that not excellent full-size successes want to be celebrated even as highlighting abilties and accomplishments. Every success and attempt, no matter how minor, need to be praised. A infant's self-self perception can be cultivated and their willingness to in reality take delivery of their particular competencies may be endorsed thru the usage of caregivers with the aid of way of using highlighting their appropriate tendencies and emphasizing the improvement they have made.

Caretakers can foster a way of life that honors and celebrates a little one's accomplishments thru way of usually pointing them out. Minors who acquire this sort of encouragement discover ways to consider of their very personal competencies and the talents of others, which strengthens their not unusual resilience and self-self guarantee.

They want to revel in confident in themselves; consequently, it is critical to create an surroundings that helps achievement and mastery. It's essential to incorporate them in hobbies wherein they can flourish, whether or not or not this is in academics, athletics, the humanities, or exceptional pastimes. Success offers youngsters extra self-self assurance and encourages them to address new duties.

If a little one expresses interest in soccer, as an example, registering them in a league may be extremely good. As a prevent end result, they are able to beautify continuously and artwork with their teammates to assemble their self notion and skills. As they broaden and reap milestones, offer useful complaint and encourage their development. Praise their accomplishments and efforts on the equal time as stressing the significance of difficult paintings and determination.

Caretakers can inspire them to growth self-self perception and a belief in their capability with the aid of the use of giving them possibilities to succeed. Positive spillover outcomes from fulfillment in a single location may want to probably encourage them to tackle new obligations with zeal and resilience. In the forestall, this promotes a increase mentality and a readiness to assist non-public improvement and lifelong reading.

One of the only approaches to assist them expand self-self guarantee is to promote healthy danger-taking. This includes encouraging them to go away their comfort zones and take delivery of troubles that check their limits. They can acquire resilience and benefit a robust enjoy of self-self guarantee thru being endorsed to attempt new topics and address tough duties.

Youngsters have to be taught that errors are amazing learning reviews and an inevitable element of improvement. Caretakers can train them that setbacks and disasters aren't indicators in their well really worth or potential via rephrasing mistakes as opportunities for development. Encourage a increase thoughts-set in them and take a look at failures as opportunities for studying.

Regardless of the outcome, parents and guardians want to applaud the braveness and difficult artwork that the kids displayed in taking over those traumatic conditions. Caretakers reaffirm the concept that self notion relies upon no longer simplest on achievement however additionally at the willingness to attempt to have a look at from evaluations through praising their bravery and spotting their efforts. This method encourages resilience and self-self assurance in the members.

Caretakers provide them with the equipment they need to discover their functionality, discover new competencies, and recover from their fears and concerns thru selling wholesome threat-taking. It aids inside the increase in their arrogance and notion in their potential to deal with novel and hard events. In the end, this could growth their self-warranty and gives them the assets they want to face up to life's u.S.And downs.

By the use of those strategies, mother and father and special adults who take care of minors can assist them end up extra self-assured, confident in their competencies, and able to deal with bullying conditions. It's important to keep in mind that growing self-self belief is a non-forestall tool that necessitates steady manual and encouragement.

The strategies that paintings for one little one won't be effective for some different because of the truth each little one is super. It is essential to alter those techniques to satisfy the particular desires and personalities of every. Maintain open strains of conversation, be aware of your youngsters' worries, and create a sturdy region for them to unique themselves.

Developing Assertiveness and Effective Communication Skills

Assertiveness and proper communique abilities are powerful device that permit children to say their limitations, articulate their wishes, and upward push as much as bullying with self assurance. By training them the ones capabilities, we give them the ability to negotiate tough conditions, form proper relationships, and suggest for themselves and others. In this phase, we're able to check practical processes for education children assertiveness and top communique competencies, further to realistic techniques for dealing with bullying.

Teaching assertiveness strategies to children is an critical step in the direction of empowering them to unique themselves hopefully and responsibly. We can assist them navigate social conditions and effectively endorse for their wishes via imparting them with realistic strategies to decorate their assertiveness competencies.

Role-playing sports activities sports are a fantastic way for them to workout competitive responses. By supplying them with numerous scenarios, together with experiencing peer pressure to engage in harmful behavior, we permit them the possibility to assertively say "no" and rise up for themselves. Role-gambling the ones situations gives them self assurance in their capacity to implement their limits and make choices which might be regular with their values.

It's crucial to train them the importance of setting up boundaries. We supply younger ones the confidence to articulate their wishes and alternatives via assisting them in recognizing their private boundaries and encouraging them to achieve this in an assertive way via using the use of expressions like "I am now not cushty with that" or "Please recognize my personal location." They can manipulate social situations with guarantee and assertiveness if it is emphasised that setting barriers is a healthful element of self-care and self-recognize.

Fostering assertiveness requires supporting them locate their voices. It is beneficial for youngsters to develop a revel in of self-expression if you encourage them to take part in conversations, ask questions, and voice their critiques. They can revel in heard and showed on the equal time as a steady, welcoming environment that appreciates and respects their evaluations is created, which will increase their self-confidence in assertively expressing themselves. They increase greater self assurance in speakme up in quite a few instances once they apprehend that their wishes and reviews rely.

Children may additionally decorate their relationships and improve their communique talents by way of manner of actively listening, this is an important aspect of right communique. By placing a strong emphasis at the want for energetic listening, empathy, and know-how, we offer them with the crucial property for lasting interactions. Here are a few effective techniques for developing children's active listening talents:

Take notice: Kids need to be intentionally recommended to be aware about the speaker. Teach them the fee of retaining eye contact, setting away telephones and unique distractions, and in reality taking note of what's being said. Those who actively pay attention to others display respect for them and affirm their tales, which conjures up openness and agree with of their interactions.

Empathy and expertise: Teach them to place themselves in different human beings's shoes to assist them increase empathy. Encourage them to consider the speaker's desires, emotions, and mindset. They can also hook up with others extra consequences and feature more significant and compassionate conversations if we help them boom the concept of empathy. This empathic mind-set additionally encourages appreciate for each other and lessens misunderstandings.

Having an empathic response: Encourage them to answer with empathy via modeling it for them. Teach them expressions like "I recognize the manner you experience" and "I apprehend that have to were difficult for you." By responding with empathy, they assist to create a supportive and being worried conversation surroundings. They inspire a experience of comfort and recollect of their interactions through demonstrating to others that their emotions are reputable and acknowledged.

Children ought to moreover have the capability to settle troubles assertively and amicably at the manner to foster wholesome relationships and prevent violent or bullying conduct. We will now study some sensible methods that could encourage them to clear up conflicts in a great manner.

Emphasize growing a deal and negotiating. Teaching them the need for compromise and negotiation in dispute preference is a useful tactic. Minors take a look at the fee of cooperation and setting up not unusual ground through being endorsed to search for win-win solutions wherein every occasions' desires are addressed. They can practice brainstorming modern mind and cultivating a cooperative mind-set through taking thing in feature-gambling severa struggle selection conditions.

Teaching them to apply "I" statements to supply their desires and emotions is every unique effective technique. Such statements embody "I revel in upset at the same time as you talk to me that way" and "I need you to pay attention to me when I am speakme." They may be competitive at the same time as specializing in their private wishes and reviews via the usage of "I" statements. This approach fosters powerful verbal exchange and emphasizes energetic listening and empathy even as lowering defensiveness.

Encourage them to maintain their hobby at the current-day-day trouble a very good way to treatment conflicts in a wholesome manner. It's essential to instill in youngsters the significance of maintaining off blame or private attacks in prefer of coping with problems head-on. They broaden respectful and answer-centered techniques to dispute choice by using way of being recommended to emphasize data the hassle and searching out solutions. This makes it feasible for them to cooperate so that you can efficiently remedy disputes and hold goodwill.

Imagine a fight amongst minors approximately who receives to play with a toy. They are advised to quietly deal with the issue and offer interest to springing up with a solution together in region of yelling or appearing violently. They examine to talk their mind, pay attention to one another, and offer you with modern techniques to percent the toy or take turns with the useful resource of receiving route and encouragement. They are able to settle their battle of phrases amicably and keep their friendship by way of manner of the usage of hammering home the significance of retaining their interest on the trouble.

Effective communique and the improvement of empathy additionally intently depend upon nonverbal communique, which includes frame language and facial emotions. It is crucial to develop kid's expertise of the relevance of nonverbal cues and their capacity to successfully interpret them. Here are some beneficial hints for fostering nonverbal verbal exchange capabilities:

Body Language: Teach them the importance of the use of open and uplifting frame language. To decorate their communication, exhort them to keep eye touch, stand or sit up straight, and use the right gestures. In order to assist them be more assertive of their relationships with others, emphasize how nonverbal clues may be used to successfully carry their mind and emotions.

Interpreting Nonverbal Cues: Encourage them to boom their capability to decipher others' nonverbal messages. In order to choose out underlying feelings and emotions, teach them to differentiate facial expressions, body postures, and speech tones. Those who very very own this capability can communicate extra effectively and meaningfully by using the use of responding to others with empathy.

Engage children in sports that encourage nonverbal communique abilties as a sensible software program. Encourage them to take part in function-gambling wearing activities in which they may exercise interpreting nonverbal clues and using right frame language, for example. To assist them in enhancing their comprehension and alertness of those capabilities, provide them with advice and awesome comments.

Give concrete examples of nonverbal expressions in various contexts. Talk about how someone's crossed fingers and wrinkled forehead have to suggest ache or struggle of words, whilst a nice smile and a cushty posture might possibly convey friendliness and openness. Minors may also additionally have a deeper data of the subtle nuances of nonverbal conversation and enhance their capability to decipher the messages they come across through emphasizing the ones examples.

Practice Empathy: Explain how nonverbal clues can show facts about the feelings and viewpoints of others to make the connection amongst nonverbal conversation and empathy. They ought to be endorsed to speculate approximately each distinctive man or woman's feelings based on their body language and facial expressions. Encourage conversations that promote empathy, which includes thinking about how numerous nonverbal signs and symptoms would probably have an effect on how we connect and speak with human beings.

Reinforcement and Encouragement: When they display off powerful nonverbal verbal exchange capabilities, improve them frequently and in a pleasing way. Celebrate their accomplishments and efforts, emphasizing the price of nonverbal cues in helping humans understand every other and forging deeper connections.

Encouraging Empathy and Kindness Towards Others

A robust feeling of belonging, healthy connections, and the ability to be compassionate are all crucial inclinations that may combat bullying. By selling kindness and empathy in youngsters, we foster a climate of decency and appreciate that no longer nice curbs bullying but additionally improves widespread nicely-being. In this segment, we will have a look at sensible strategies for schooling them kindness and empathy as a way to enhance their interpersonal interactions and the groups wherein they stay.

Modeling Empathy

When we exemplify empathy in our personal conduct, it encourages kids to exercise empathy, this is quite useful. By displaying empathy and data in your private relationships, you could powerfully have an effect on those round you for your function as a caregiver. They recognize hearing from adults who without a doubt care about their mind and emotions. You also can assist them examine the fee of contemplating the perspectives of others via acknowledging their sentiments and responding in an empathic manner. Emphasize the significance of empathy in forming deep connections by the usage of encouraging them to position themselves in each extraordinary person's shoes earlier than passing judgment or making assumptions. They boom a stronger preserve close of the importance of empathy and are stimulated to use it to their private lives through way of listening to memories or memories that demonstrate its wonderful results.

Chapter 2: Recognizing And Dealing With Bullies

Bullying is an excessive problem that may damage kid's well-being and arrogance ultimately. They need to take delivery of the know-how and abilities to discover and reply to bullying conditions. By supporting them recognize bullying behavior and training them the manner to reply to it, we give them the self warranty they want to get up for themselves, ask for assistance from accountable adults, and inspire peaceful conflict selection. Let's have a examine those elements in greater element, offering tips and illustrations that kids and their caregivers can use in every day interactions.

Teaching Children to Identify and Handle Bullying Situations

Recognizing bullying is an essential ability for more youthful ones to research since it lets in them to deal with and reply to such conditions successfully. We empower them to guard themselves and others with the resource of coaching them to understand and respond to bullying. In this segment, we can take a look at strategies to educate them to come across bullying behavior, distinguish it from everyday struggle, and equip them with reaction options.

Understanding Bullying

Start with the aid of outlining what bullying is and the manner it varies from everyday conflicts. Bullying is defined as a series of destructive moves keen approximately the purpose to harm or dominate a victim. It is critical to underline that bullying is both intentional and unjust. Give college students examples of verbal, physical, and social bullying to help them apprehend the concept.

Name-calling, taunting, and spreading rumors are all examples of verbal bullying. Physical bullying consists of actions like kicking, pushing, or beating some other man or woman. Social bullying takes many paperwork, which include except for people, shelling out false statistics, and faking friendships. By providing concrete examples, university college students may need to have a higher knowledge of the numerous styles of bullying and the manner to understand them in real-existence occasions.

Trusting Instincts and Taking Bullying Seriously

Children want to be knowledgeable to observe their senses after they note someone being bullied or on the identical time as they may be being bullied themselves. Teach them to be aware of their feelings and physical reactions as symptoms and signs of a bullying situation. Help children recognize that any form of bullying, no matter how intense, need to be taken significantly and not disregarded as just teasing or innocent conduct.

We empower them to stand bullying effectively with the beneficial useful resource of respecting their feelings and highlighting the importance of taking movement. Teach them that asking for assistance isn't a signal of weak point however as an alternative a brave step within the course of selection. Kids have the right to experience strong and steady and it is the man or woman's project to provide the steady place.

Assertiveness and Self-Advocacy

When they are bullied, it's miles vital to arm them with assertiveness and self-advocacy techniques. Encourage them to apply assertive frame language, speak up, and demand their rights. Teach them phrases like "Stop" and "I do now not find it irresistible whilst you try this" to signify their obstacles and particular their displeasure.

By appearing out diverse bullying situations, scholars may additionally moreover take a look at forceful responses. Give instructions on a way to keep eye contact, talk in truth, and stand tall to unique self belief. Remind them that they have the proper to self-protection and that their voice subjects. We empower them to say themselves for you to set limits and arise to bullying.

Seeking Help and Reporting

It is crucial to teach them the want of attempting to find aid and reporting bullying activities for his or her very private nicely-being similarly to the general protection of the school. We empower them to take proactive efforts in the direction of addressing bullying conditions and organising a manner of lifestyles of admire and help thru extending their expertise of those thoughts.

First and essential, it's far critical to emphasise to kids that asking for help isn't a signal of frailty or complaining. They must understand that, that lets in you to defend themselves and others from chance, reporting bullying is a accountable and vital movement. Encourage them to method a reliable grownup, inclusive of a decide, trainer, or faculty counselor, with a purpose to are trying to find advice and resource. This creates a guide tool for them.

Clear commands ought to be given in order that they will apprehend who to go to for useful resource. It's critical for them to be aware about precise people they'll confide in and experience comfortable sharing their reviews with. They can have a easy direction to study even as reporting sports activities if the school's resources and assist structures, which include a committed mechanism for reporting bullying or unique employees human beings, are made express.

It's furthermore vital to foster an environment that is welcoming and approachable for you to inspire children to invite for assist. Adults should attentively be privy to younger ones, confirm their research, and provide the right steerage. Adults can also additionally inspire children to percentage their studies without demanding approximately grievance or retaliation through developing acquire as proper with and empathy in them. They will become greater confident inside the reporting method if confidentiality is maintained and each record is taken substantially.

Documentation and Evidence

In order to confront and dispose of bullying, documentation and evidence are vital. Children who are encouraged to report bullying conditions advantage the capability to take manage in their critiques and are assisted in navigating the reporting approach. They are better organized for assist or intervention at the same time as bullying episodes are documented, collectively with the date, time, area, and a entire account of what transpired. If extra movement is wanted, this documentation may be used as strong evidence, giving an in depth account of the bullying episodes and bolstering their case.

Teaching them the importance of maintaining any virtual proof of bullying in current virtual international is similarly essential. This includes keeping screenshots of offensive texts or other types of cyberbullying, which embody internet bullying. Such proof can help create a path of abusive conduct, making it less complicated to entice the offenders and take any crucial movement. By emphasizing the rate of digital evidence, they'll be recommended to guard themselves and others closer to the dangerous effects of on line bullying.

Speaking to university college students approximately the charge of reporting bullying and status up for folks which are being bullied is also key. By actively supporting their buddies who're being bullied, they'll help to create a culture of expertise and compassion of their neighborhoods. They must analyze obligation and empathy and that their movements can also have a excellent have an effect on on the lives of others. By talking out in opposition to bullying, supplying help, and reporting incidents, they make a contribution to the arrival of a stable and inclusive surroundings wherein virtually everybody feels valued and favored.

Strategies for Responding to Bullying, Including Seeking Help from Trusted Adults

To reply correctly and deal with the hassle, students must have powerful coping talents at the same time as they are subjected to bullying. We allow them to fight bullying through education them tactics together with soliciting for assist from reliable adults, encouraging non violent dispute selection, and growing a guide tool. In this section, we are able to have a examine useful techniques that children and their caregivers can use.

Seeking Help from Trusted Adults

To address the bullying problem, the ones adults can offer assistance, direction, and intervention. The following are a few techniques to train students:

Help them find out the sincere people in their lives with whom they experience confident sharing records. Parents, educators, counselors, or administrators may also fall into this elegance. Encourage them to talk overtly with those reliable human beings and pressure that they are there to assist.

Play feature-gambling video video games with them to offer them workout drawing near a dependable grownup and explaining the bullying problem. They benefit the self perception and conversation skills they want to ask for assistance because of this. Encourage them to explain the incidents in element, together with dates, instances, places, and any witnesses.

Stress the need to record precise bullying conditions to responsible humans. To provide an intensive description of each incident, inspire them to put in writing down the specifics, collectively with what changed into stated or finished. Inform adults that reporting specific instances allows them to evaluate the gravity of the problem and take the important movement.

Ensure minors that adults are in fee of handling and preventing bullying. Tell them they are no longer on my own in coping with the circumstances by using permitting them to understand that adults are there to assist them. By related to reliable adults, kids have get admission to to gear and interventions which can successfully deal with bullying.

Promoting Nonviolent Conflict Resolution and De-escalation Techniques

Responding to bullying calls for coaching greater youthful ones amazing war resolution techniques in region of aggression or violence. Here are a few techniques that encourage non violent war choice:

Encourage them to remain collected and calm inside the presence of bullies. Help them apprehend that spontaneous outbursts of rage or aggression ought to make matters worse. To regain composure before replying to the bully, recommend taking some deep breaths, counting to ten, or taking a break.

Insist that violent altercations want to be averted due to the fact they'll be unstable and possibly make the problem worse. They want to gain knowledge of to confront bullies with phrases instead of blows. Encourage them to assertively speak their wants and needs with out using pressure.

Educate them on de-escalation strategies that can be used to save you bullying. These techniques can entail leaving the vicinity, going somewhere safe, or asking buddies or exceptional dependable humans for assistance. Inform them that stepping far from the modern issue can allow them time to mirror and maintain in mind one-of-a-kind courses of motion.

If they may be now not capable of clear up a problem on their own, inspire them to are on the lookout for for mediation or consult a reliable person. Mediation can provide a independent placing for speakme about troubles and identifying factors of settlement. Involving a dependable person guarantees that the problem is well treated and that the right steps are taken.

Building a Support Network

For youngsters to experience empowered and supported in confronting bullying situations, it's far important to amplify a aid device. The following are techniques for assisting kids in growing a sturdy help tool:

Encourage them to are attempting to find out pals and peers who oppose bullying and to surround themselves with awesome influences. Encourage them to pick out companions that rate generosity, compassion, and inclusivity.

Encourage participation in activities that build excessive fine relationships and a revel in of community. Encourage them to enroll in businesses, participate in institution sports activities sports sports, or volunteer in the community. These comparable pursuits provide possibilities to form relationships based totally totally on shared ideals and pastimes.

Chapter 3: Creating A Supportive Community

Bullying is a excessive trouble which can harm children in the end. In order to efficaciously fight bullying, supportive surroundings ought to be installation that nurtures healthy connections, supports inclusive behavior, and develops empathy and understanding. The techniques for growing a supportive environment is probably stated in this section, with a focus on developing peer relationships, encouraging inclusive conduct, valuing variety, and growing empathy and information through function-playing and storytelling. Pupils and their caregivers can actively combat bullying and foster a stable and inclusive surroundings with the aid of setting those techniques into exercise.

Nurturing Positive Relationships Among Peers

In order to stop bullying and confront it, wholesome peer interactions are essential.

Those who form near bonds with their classmates revel in a enjoy of aid and belonging, which fosters a network in which bullying is much less possibly to seem. By giving youngsters the danger to engage constructively and form deep connections, teachers and one-of-a-type adults play a vital function in fostering those relationships. Exploring enterprise-constructing sports activities, collaborative tasks, group conversations, peer mentoring initiatives, and promoting extracurricular sports are some strategies for developing robust relationships among buddies.

Children can boom powerful relationships thru a laugh and a hit organization-constructing activities. They have the hazard to paintings collectively through the ones sports activities activities which sell trust, communique, and cooperation. One exquisite instance is a teacher-organized scavenger hunt wherein college college students cooperate to decipher clues and locate hid devices. These sports assist them construct crucial social skills on the identical time as concurrently encouraging teamwork.

During institution-constructing wearing activities, they've a look at the importance of collaboration as they paintings collectively to advantage a commonplace aim. They suddenly apprehend that via pooling their assets, they're capable to carry out extra than they could on their non-public. They are stimulated through this interest to actively engage in peer verbal exchange, share thoughts, and assist the achievement of the group. Through cooperation, minors examine the importance of collective trouble-solving and experience its power.

Furthermore, team-building physical sports activities foster a spirit of friendship and crew spirit among university students. Those who collaborate together construct consider and rely on every different for manual. They look at the benefits of help, delegated responsibilities, and effective communication. Because in their commonplace reviews, classmates come to be in the direction of each other, fostering a nice and alluring studying surroundings.

Those who take part in crew-building bodily video video games now not handiest have a observe the price of walking collectively however additionally enlarge vital social capabilities. They learn how to control agency dynamics, interact in lively listening, and speak efficaciously. These competencies beautify their relationships in loads of contexts, which consist of academic partnerships, friendships, and upcoming group-based totally duties, and bypass beyond the hobby itself.

Cooperative tasks moreover provide kids useful possibilities to paintings collectively at the same time as fusing their precise skills and viewpoints. Teachers and caregivers might assign cooperative institution assignments like planning a class fundraiser or portray a mural collectively. Kids benefit an information of the numerous skills and skills in their friends through those tasks.

The fulfillment of the venture relies upon on the efforts of each institution member, each of whom has a tremendous function to play. Working together educates them to understand every different's mind and abilities, fostering an inclusive environment wherein genuinely every person feels supported.

Cooperative obligations provide children with critical life competencies which include powerful conversation, negotiating, and hassle-fixing. They have to broaden the functionality to cope with disagreements and conquer obstacles as a set. Through this technique, youngsters look at the talents crucial for fostering healthful relationships and averting disputes, which includes listening, negotiating, and finding not unusual floor.

Group talks are each special powerful method for education them to talk their mind, relate their research, and take examine of every distinct. By fostering open discussions on awesome topics like empathy, friendship, and appreciate, instructors and caregivers can also foster a steady and alluring environment. Children are taught to reflect and bear in mind crucial issues through being asked probing questions like, "How can we be kinder to each other?" or "Why is it important to include absolutely everyone?"

Youngsters have the threat to voice their reviews and emotions thru organization conversations, which promotes a greater records of each other. They get the ability to actively pay attention whilst respecting and appreciating the reviews and stories in their peers. As a prevent stop result, peer relationships are reinforced, and a solid help network is created within the school or community. This fosters empathy and develops a feel of oneness.

Additionally, group conversations help youngsters become higher communicators as they learn how to nicely and successfully specific their mind. They examine the way to speak effectively, participate in conversations, and react to exquisite human beings's thoughts. These verbal exchange competencies are crucial for growing healthy connections and non violent struggle choice.

Programs for peer mentoring have moreover been demonstrated to be powerful strategies that assist every older and extra younger students. These applications deliver older university students the chance to mentor their extra more youthful pals, fostering a way of existence of responsibility, compassion, and control. Older college college students function mentors for more youthful college

college college students, giving them recommendation, camaraderie, and help.

In a software program of peer mentorship, older college students can help their extra younger opposite numbers in plenty of techniques. They must offer educational resource, tutoring, or help with coursework. Additionally, they might provide steerage in overcoming social limitations like making friends or resolving disputes. Being a welcoming presence can occasionally make a big effect on a greater younger student's existence with the useful resource of encouraging a enjoy of assist and belonging.

Students construct a experience of resource and trust in the university network thru taking detail in applications for peer mentorship. Peers are capable of find out with the issues and troubles that one of a kind college college college students face, making it much less tough for younger college university students to technique peer mentors for recommendation and assist. In turn, as they address the location of mentor, older college college students growth a stronger revel in of obligation and empathy. Along with mastering the manner to be affected person and kind to their more younger pals, further they benefit management developments.

Taking element in extracurricular sports activities activities extensively contributes to the improvement of terrific relationships amongst peers. These sports, consisting of turning into a member of a sports activities activities group, taking issue in art work groups, or acting community carrier, convey youngsters together based on similar hobbies. Teachers and unique adults who deal with youngsters can encourage them to investigate tremendous extracurricular sports activities activities and guide their participation. Through the ones sports sports, kids can engage with specific youngsters who percentage their interests, make friends, and discover a experience of network.

A various and inclusive community wherein man or woman abilties and strengths are respected is promoted via extracurricular sports. Kids interact with others who percentage their pastimes as soon as they have interaction in sports they revel in. A student who enjoys portray, for example, should be a part of an art work group and meet wonderful folks who percentage that interest. The basis for forming friendships and wholesome peer connections is that this shared ardour.

In addition to fostering social bonds, the ones sports moreover provide a nurturing surroundings that lessens the possibility of bullying. In extracurricular sports activities, they frequently practice teamwork, collaboration, and inexperienced verbal exchange. They benefit information approximately the fee of collaboration, apprehend, and empathy thru taking

44

component in business enterprise projects or organization-based totally activities. Bullying is a lot a whole lot less likely to arise on this supportive environment because it fosters cooperation, appreciation for difference, and a feel of community.

Teachers and caregivers also can create a network free of bullying with the useful resource of putting those techniques into workout and inspiring right connections amongst friends. They are more equipped to confront bullies and rise up for each different even as teamwork, cooperation, conversation, and empathy are promoted through extracurricular sports, cooperative responsibilities, employer discussions, peer mentorship packages, and team-building sporting activities. Together, permit's create a warm, welcoming space in which every infant can enjoy valued, legit, and steady.

Encouraging Inclusive Behavior and Celebrating Differences

Making an accepting environment in which every body feels valued and revered requires selling inclusion and embracing range. In order to prevent bullying and promote a experience of belonging, it's miles vital to train kids to clearly receive range and address absolutely everyone with love and apprehend, regardless of what their heritage, capability, or seems can be. Let's test some ability and particular strategies to have a laugh range and sell inclusive behavior with children and their caregivers.

Highlighting the Value of Diversity

In the study room or at domestic, educators and caregivers play a vital function in emphasizing the significance of range to children. We can amplify their horizons and inspire inclusion via providing teachings and conversations that emphasize the price of range. Educating them approximately famous humans from many cultures who have made amazing contributions to society is an powerful approach. For example, they may find out about historic human beings like Mahatma Gandhi and Frida Kahlo, or scientists like Marie Curie. They will have a have a look at at once approximately the richness that variety gives to our international thru paying attention to tales and anecdotes approximately those humans.

Diverse literature, films, and portions of art must be covered into the studying environment in addition to emphasizing person accomplishments. Through this publicity, they could see each themselves and awesome human beings depicted, encouraging inclusion and deepening their information of numerous viewpoints. Artwork that displays a couple of ingenious traditions, films which have a take a look at specific cultures, and books with protagonists from numerous origins can all assist foster an inclusive surroundings. These assets supply youngsters the hazard to engage with severa memories and reports, which fosters empathy and a more expertise of the importance of variety.

Challenging Stereotypes

Stereotypes are routinely provided to minors in a number of contexts, which includes the media, interpersonal interactions, and personal evaluations. It is essential to set up a secure, welcoming environment wherein they'll talk and freely refute the ones misconceptions. The duty of educators and caregivers to sell conversations that sell important wondering and talk to into question stereotypes is important.

Sharing examples from real lifestyles or reminiscences that defy prejudice is a powerful technique. These reminiscences can shed slight on folks who defy stereotypes and society's norms. Children have a extra nuanced reputation of numerous cultures, competencies, and identities while exposed to quite some narratives. It motivates college students to look past apparent presumptions and admire the complexity of humans and companies.

It's critical to inspire them to invite questions and look for real records that permits you to combat stereotypes. By encouraging interest, educators and caregivers permit them the freedom to research many viewpoints and study new subjects. This fosters a weather wherein preconceptions can be overcome and empathy can amplify. By fostering a more empathetic and sympathetic perspective, kids are capable of confront prejudices and deal with human beings pretty.

Promoting Empathy and Understanding

Empathy and information need to be cultivated as a way to amplify an inclusive manner of lifestyles wherein everyone feels favored and respected. Children can develop empathy through a number of sports that educators and caregivers may also moreover use. Role-playing video games that allow children positioned themselves in other human beings's shoes and experience various emotions and factors of view is one inexperienced method. Kids can better understand the difficulties that new college students, humans with disabilities, and those from special cultural backgrounds can also come across on a normal foundation by using manner of taking turns gambling those roles.

Through function-playing, they learn how to reply with love and facts, while also growing a better consciousness of variety. They start to realise that everybody has certainly one of a kind research and emotions, which lets in dispel prejudices and growth empathy. Role-playing allows children learn how to undergo in thoughts and articulate the mind and emotions of the characters they painting, which moreover promotes lively listening and suitable communique.

Through the ones sports sports in empathy-building, they benefit useful competencies that assist set up greater inclusive groups. They discover ways to charge others' variations and are better able to recognize and understand their individual tendencies. In the give up, encouraging empathy and knowledge helps them locate the power to confront bullying and decorate a more compassionate and welcoming community.

Organizing Events and Projects

Activities and responsibilities that maintain in mind considered one in every of a type cultures, customs, and skills may be extraordinarily beneficial to a child. These applications and duties help to sell tolerance and variety. They gain appreciably from the opportunities furnished by way of manner of educators and caregivers once they prepare multicultural festivals, art famous, or expertise indicates.

The fact that each one children are advised to take part within the ones sports activities fosters inclusivity and a enjoy of success. By sharing their cultural statistics, traditions, or talents, they advantage a broader facts of numerous cultures at the same time as furthermore turning into extra aware in their private.

Chapter 4: Cyber Bullying Awareness

In cutting-edge day digitally advanced, globally associated global, cyberbullying has improved to a huge fear. Online bullying can have a devastating impact, inflicting extreme emotional struggling and in all likelihood extended-term intellectual damage. It is critical to growth recognition of cyberbullying and deliver human beings the device they need to fight it if we are going to forestall this developing trouble. An in-depth speak of the dangers of on line harassment, an emphasis on particular digital citizenship and on-line protection, and a focus at the significance of reporting and getting help at the identical time as confronted with cyberbullying are all topics included on this section.

Understanding the Dangers of Online Harassment and Cyberbullying

Because it has spread in some unspecified time in the future of many digital channels, cyberbullying is a chronic and sneaky shape of online harassment that exposes its patients to quite some nefarious actions. It involves dispensing unfaithful statistics, posting comments on social media internet web sites as an example, developing fictitious profiles, and disclosing personal records with out permission in an effort to embarrass or damage others. These violent acts can take place in masses of on line settings, collectively with well-known social media web sites, personal messaging offerings, on line gaming organizations, or even email exchanges.

Cyberbullying sufferers might also moreover have horrible and lengthy-lasting consequences that have an impact on them in every their every day lives and the net international. Due to emotional aspect effects which incorporates despair, anxiety, and occasional conceitedness, a victim's highbrow fitness might also furthermore undergo extensively. Intense emotions of helplessness and hopelessness can give up result from the onslaught of nasty comments and on line attacks, making sufferers doubt their charge and undermining their self belief. Because of this, sufferers frequently feel on my own and withdraw socially, locating it more difficult and tougher to assemble great relationships. Tragically, because of the acute intellectual struggling that cyberbullying reasons, a few patients may moreover even start having suicidal thoughts or start harming themselves.

Beyond just emotional misery, cyberbullying could have a essential bad have an impact on on on a sufferer's personal and academic lives. Their capability to awareness on their studies can be disrupted with the resource of the regular harassment, that could motive analyzing troubles and a discount in academic overall performance. Further separating patients from their resource systems is the continuing fear and tension added on via cyberbullying, that might make sufferers become bored in formerly preferred sports activities activities, pursuits, and social interactions. These setbacks also can have lengthy-term results on their educational paths and dim their possibilities for a successful career.

The ease of anonymity offered with the resource of online structures is one of the crucial barriers to stopping cyberbullying. Cyberbullying perpetrators regularly cowl their proper identities and keep away from responsibility for their crimes via the usage of digital masks. This experience of anonymity gives cyberbullies the liberty to harm others with out disturbing approximately going via on the spot repercussions. A vital first step in effectively stopping cyberbullying is exposing the ones offenders and protecting them responsible. Communities may also additionally make it obvious that such behavior will not be usual through figuring out and exposing folks which can be inside the back of on-line abuse.

Because their actions have the power to either beef up or spoil the cycle of harm, bystanders play a vital position in the dynamics of cyberbullying. Bystanders who passively have a have a take a look at or, worse yet, actively take part in cyberbullying help to maintain the poor on line climate alive. Bystanders can, however, moreover step in and exchange topics for the better. By attractive bystanders to talk out in the direction of cyberbullying, we are able to assemble a steady and welcoming on line surroundings in which bullies are a lot plenty less probably to acquire achievement. Bystanders' capability to document incidents of cyberbullying, manual sufferers, and communicate out in the direction of on-line harassment can help trade the steadiness of power and create a compassionate, empathic, and resilient environment.

It is important to provide beneficial steerage and feasible actions that may be positioned into exercising on a every day basis so one can control cyberbullying successfully and defend minors and their caregivers. Children need to acquire early steering on on-line protection and unique digital citizenship. Building empathy and compassion in kids starts with instructing them approximately appropriate on line conduct, the dangers of cyberbullying, and the value of treating others with love and admire. They ought to also be given useful advice on safeguarding their personal facts, identifying cyberbullying caution signs and signs, and getting to know the manner to react and get assist whilst faced with on-line harassment.

In order to combat cyberbullying, caregivers need to furthermore play a key function. It is critical for mother and father to keep the traces of verbal exchange open with their infants an outstanding way to actively listen to their problems, phobias, and internet critiques. Caregivers can higher keep close the dangers and help their college students develop healthful on-line behavior by manner of getting involved with and studying approximately the digital structures their youngsters use. Essential safeguards encompass putting in clean commands for steady on-line behavior, putting barriers, and constantly checking up on their kids' on line sports.

Caretakers can pressure the rate of empathy, kindness, and inclusion in every the web and offline worlds, similarly to prevention and response. Building a tradition of brotherly love and resilience amongst youngsters includes schooling them to talk out in opposition to cyberbullying and to help sufferers. They can also moreover help create a more strong and extra compassionate online surroundings with the resource of being actively worried in promoting super on line interactions, reporting times of cyberbullying, and building a sense of community.

Teaching Responsible Digital Citizenship and Online Safety

It is crucial to offer youngsters and their caregivers greater certain information, anecdotes, examples, and beneficial steering that encourages responsible digital citizenship and on-line protection. This will help fight cyberbullying extra successfully.

Respect and empathy are the cornerstones of moral digital citizenship. Interactive sporting sports that foster empathy can be protected into coaching strategies and family talks thru educators, dad and mom, and other caregivers. For example, they will plan group sports in which minors collaborate to recognize and speak approximately the feelings of someone who has been a sufferer of cyberbullying. They can gain a better maintain near of the consequences in their terms and behaviors on-line thru placing themselves in amazing people's footwear.

Educators and caregivers can percent personal money owed of patients of cyberbullying and the effects it has. These money owed could in all likelihood function a reminder of the emotional toll that cyberbullying exacts on its patients and the long-lasting damage that it is able to cause. Anecdotes can also display the tenacity and fortitude of those who have triumphed over cyberbullying, motivating them to oppose it and communicate up for folks that are the dreams.

Critical questioning abilties and media literacy are important equipment for navigating the net securely. Teachers can upload fingers-on activities to their training to teach college college students a manner to compare online content material cloth fabric severely. For instance, they're able to provide illustrations of news memories or social media posts and train students on a manner to reality-check, locate truthful property, and be aware biases or faux facts. They can discover ways to confirm the reliability and accuracy of the records they stumble upon with the useful resource of getting conversations with them about on line content cloth.

Security and privateness protections are critical components of moral digital citizenship. They can look at beneficial techniques from educators, parents, and extraordinary adults for protecting their non-public information online. They can provide commands on a way to regulate privacy settings on social networking net websites and emphasize the fee of shielding clients' non-public records. By paying attention to recollections or examples of situations whilst sharing non-public records caused terrible results, they may have a observe the importance of prudence. By offering them with beneficial recommendation like developing consistent passwords which are each robust and unique and abstaining from sharing private records on line with strangers, parents can also additionally moreover empower their youngsters to take proactive steps to maintain their privacy.

To create a helpful on line network, one want to first set up top notch on line relationships. Young ones can get maintain of sensible guidance from educators and caregivers on the way to join without a doubt online. For instance, they may be taught the importance of giving compliments, expressing thanks, and supporting out their friends. Hearing testimonies about or seeing instances of on line agencies in which kindness and help are commonplace may additionally additionally encourage humans to make a contribution to a first-rate on-line environment. Role-gambling situations or corporation conversations can help to emphasise how vital it's miles to fight on-line abuse and expand inclusivity and kindness.

By imparting practical techniques for dealing with cyberbullying, mother and father can deliver their youngsters the self perception to take fee and ask for assist when they want it. Teachers and parents can also additionally offer whole instructions on the way to record instances of cyberbullying and accumulate proof. To show off how the reporting strategies which might be available on various on line structures function, they may be in a role to make use of images or motion photos. With the assist of particular instructions, collectively with refraining from revenge or enticing the cyberbully, they'll test the significance of protective their very very personal well-being. Additionally, caregivers can stress the price of requesting help from reliable folks that can provide course and assist, collectively with teachers, mother and father, or faculty counselors.

Educators and caregivers can also emphasize the price of speaking up in area of being silent. Children will have a examine from them how their movements can assist save you cyberbullying. They may be empowered to actively make contributions to a way of life of empathy and concord with the aid of the usage of being attentive to and appearing on sensible advice, which encompass providing help to sufferers, reporting abusive behavior, or speakme out against on line harassment. Real-world examples or accounts of humans who've acted to help sufferers or unfold positivity on-line also can feature idea.

Addressing the Importance of Reporting and Seeking Help

Raising consciousness of the problem of cyberbullying is crucial, however so is giving human beings the strength to attain this through reporting incidents of on-line harassment. In order to prevent cyberbullying, reporting is important because it lets in sufferers, onlookers, and witnesses to perform that in competition to the offenders. Individuals can also prevent cyberbullying and boost a safer online environment via being privy to the reporting options on many on-line systems, including social media, gaming systems, and messaging apps.

Chapter 5: Promoting Up-Stander Culture

The prevalence of bullying, discrimination, and harassment in extremely-current society makes it vital to inspire an upstanding subculture. An up-stander is a person who actively tries to create a strong and inclusive ecosystem, stands up for folks which can be being bullied, and opposes injustice. This chapter seeks to offer useful suggestions and techniques for encouraging children to talk up for others, cultivating a sense of civic obligation, and growing a solid surroundings for all.

Empowering Children as Up-standers

Empowering youngsters to end up up-standers is a critical step in cultivating empathy, kindness, and apprehend. Rather than being passive bystanders, they might boom the confidence and abilities important to interfere and help their pals. Let's find out realistic strategies to empower them as up-standers.

Education and Awareness

Education and know-how play an important function in empowering youngsters to be up-standers. Through training, they are capable of advantage the vital know-how and facts about empathy, compassion, and the bad consequences of bullying. We can provide them with the tool they need to end up active up-standers via encouraging open conversations and imparting age-appropriate belongings.

Schools, dad and mom, and agencies all have the responsibility of teaching them on the price of empathy and data. Pupils can gain a higher records of the electricity dynamics concerned in bullying conditions with the useful resource of along side those mind inside the curriculum and appealing in vast discussions. They observe that being silent can motive harm and contribute to a lousy surroundings.

Inviting visitor audio system who have skilled bullying and changed into up-standers is a wonderful way to promote training and recognition. These people can share their personal reminiscences, discussing the troubles they professional and the alternatives they made to indicate for themselves and others. Students can join emotionally, empathize with the speaker's journey, and maintain near the importance of their feature as up-standers thru listening to about real-life studies.

Guest audio device display how empathy, resilience, and braveness should make a distinction. They display that everybody, regardless of ancient beyond or scenario, has the potential to impact powerful exchange. These audio gadget' personal tales may also have a profound have an impact on on kids, pushing them to accomplish that and arise to bullying of their very personal lives.

Additionally, age-appropriate belongings alongside aspect books, movies, and interactive sports can help them understand empathy and upstanding behavior. These belongings can present numerous factors of view, cope with numerous types of bullying, and provide practical intervention answers. Children can actively take part of their mastering and accumulate a stronger feeling of empathy for others by the use of exciting materials.

Building Self-self perception

Self-self assure development is a crucial difficulty in empowering kids to end up up-standers. Strongly self-assured kids are more likely to take initiative and shield others while faced with challenges. Their arrogance can be considerably boosted by way of using being taught to admire their very very own developments, capabilities, and competencies, if you want to permit them to cope with difficult social conditions with conviction and empathy.

Teaching kids a way to govern conflicts gently and assertively is an vital part of developing their self-self warranty. It is essential to emphasize that struggle selection does no longer always require struggle of phrases however can alternatively be achieved through first-rate communique and problem-solving. By arming youngsters with these property, they will be able to confront bullying situations with self notion and a choice to make a difference.

Practical sports, collectively with characteristic-playing sporting activities, are useful for growing self-self warranty. These bodily sports activities offer a stable and supportive putting for children to exercising sticking up for someone who is being bullied. They can broaden the abilities needed to intervene efficaciously, talk their issues assertively, and offer help to people in need thru modeling actual-existence events.

During role-gambling sports, kids can tackle severa roles, which include the up-stander, the bullied man or woman, or even the bystander. This lets in university college students to obtain a better records of the dynamics at paintings, similarly to the capability consequences of their moves. By taking component in those simulations, college students come to be greater familiar with the emotions and boundaries related with intervening in bullying conditions, which enhances their shallowness.

It is also critical to offer great comments and exceptional reinforcement at some point of these obligations. By looking at and appreciating their efforts and a achievement intervention strategies, caregivers and educators can decorate their self-confidence and inspire them to preserve being up-standers in actual-existence conditions.

It is important to apprehend that developing self-self notion is an ongoing manner that necessitates everyday encouragement and help. In an environment in which caregivers and instructors are supportive, children need to experience comfortable expressing themselves, asking questions, and discovering their very very own specific competencies. When a supportive and inclusive environment is developed, they are more likely to broaden a sturdy enjoy of self-worth, letting them encompass their characteristic as up-standers and characteristic a very good impact on their groups.

Developing Empathy

Empathy is an important characteristic of up-standers. Minors must learn how to placed themselves inside the shoes of others, come to be aware of the emotional impact of bullying, and understand the importance of reputation up for folks that are mistreated. Storytelling, role-gambling bodily activities, and inspiring mind-set-taking sports can assist educators and mother and father sell empathy.

Teachers, for instance, can study novels or show movies depicting people in bullying situations. Following that, youngsters can interact in discussions approximately the characters' research, sharing their views and feelings. This pastime lets in children construct empathy and emphasizes the concept of helping others.

Chapter 6: Developing Resilience

Resilience is a key lifestyles trait that enables young ones to stand as an awful lot as adversity, recover from tough testimonies, and thrive within the face of adversity. In this economic catastrophe, we're capable of have a examine three important additives of fostering resilience in kids: assisting them in convalescing from bullying reviews, setting up coping capabilities and emotional resilience, and promoting a increase mind-set and a high-quality outlook. They can construct the system they want to barter the us of americaand downs of life with self belief and electricity thru focusing on those regions.

Helping Children Bounce Back From Bullying Experiences

Bullying might also moreover have a huge terrible effect on a little one's well-being, arrogance, and fashionable resilience. It is essential for caregivers to create a secure and supportive surroundings that allows open communique. Establishing a normal "check-in" time together at the side of your little one when they'll brazenly communicate their mind and emotions with out fear of judgment is one practical technique to carry out this. This provides an opportunity for them to reveal any bullying evaluations they will have had.

In the scenario so as to be cited, a extra younger character has to address the distressing enjoy of bullying at school. In the face of the distressing scenario, they obtained help and knowledge from their mother and father, who took care to emphasise their commitment to being there for his or her infant thru thick and thin via presenting a sympathetic ear and reassurance when they located of their toddler's problems.

The mother and father had been proactive in addressing the trouble in a effective way. They communicated with the directors of the college and labored together to discover a solution. They set up a assembly with the instructor and the steering counselor, which supplied a venue for an in-depth talk of the hassle. They collaborated to provide you with a course of motion to shield their child's safety and well-being at the identical time as attending college.

The dad and mom' behavior discovered out their steadfast determination to imparting a steady and nurturing surroundings for their little one's growth and improvement. In addition to addressing the right away trouble of bullying, moreover they emphasised a deeper strength of will to organising a steady and provoking surroundings in which their infant may develop and broaden. Their participation and help tested to the teen that they have got been not by myself of their worrying conditions and that their parents have been there to look out for and resource them alongside the manner.

Aside from addressing the winning state of affairs, caregivers can assist children in growing assertiveness competencies. Use "I" statements to educate them a manner to talk their feelings and establish obstacles. Encourage your child, as an instance, to specific, "I experience harm at the identical time as you assert advocate subjects to me, and I need you to prevent." By coaching them assertiveness competencies, they may regain control of the scenario and actively have interaction in resolving it.

We will now take a look at a scenario wherein a more youthful character is subjected to verbal abuse through a classmate to further make clean the argument made above. The toddler's parents determine to empower them with the useful resource of offering assertiveness abilities in reaction to this demanding conduct.

The dad and mom' method includes taking part in interactive sports that imitate diverse bullying eventualities. They train their toddler to apply "I" statements to answer assertively at a few level inside the ones sports if you need to efficiently particular their emotions and perspectives. The parents art work with their toddler to offer you with and exercise empowering terms to say when confronted with bullying.

Their infant profits a number of self-self perception and empowerment because of this encouraging advise. They gain the capacity to mention themselves with self belief and communicate their feelings and thoughts more genuinely. As a quit result, the bullies discover that as time passes, their tries to torment the younger individual end up a lot less powerful. The toddler's newly obtained assertiveness permits an environment wherein they'll higher keep their emotional well-being and negotiate such tough conditions with resilience.

To useful aid in their recovery from bullying, encourage scholars to create a network of type buddies. Through involvement in extracurricular sports activities like group sports activities sports, clubs, or network agencies, they may connect with classmates who percentage their values of compassion and inclusion. These relationships can offer individuals help, boosting their resilience and sense of self esteem.

Imagine a teenager who loves the humanities and well-knownshows pride in her creative endeavors. Her dad and mom want her to join the college's art membership due to the fact they virtually useful aid her pastimes. She takes the opportunity and meets awesome artwork fanatics who're interested by the same topics she is. Her robust relationships with the opposite artists inside the company help to create a experience of community. Their ties are further reinforced by way of way of walking together on numerous duties and showing their collective creativity. Her friends provide a critical useful resource community at the same time as she encounters bullying. She shares her reports, asks for advice, and finds emotional consolation through open conversation, empowering her to face tough conditions with resiliency and assurance.

As caregivers, it's miles vital to instill the values of empathy and kindness in young ones. To lend a listening ear or a assisting hand to classmates who are being bullied or who're feeling lonely, they want to discover ways to make eye touch with them. By fostering an mind-set of compassion and inclusiveness, they learn how to create a splendid and inspiring surroundings that discourages bullying behavior.

The emphasis right right here is on a tremendous act of empathy and kindness executed in a social context. One person notices that some other individual is mechanically bullied and saved away from through their friends. The observer addresses the hassle right away in preference to acting as a passive bystander. They determine to become friends with the outcast, inviting them to enroll in in on institution sports activities and characteristic lunch together. The observer might not prevent there; similarly they communicate out to result in others to be kind and accepting closer to the ostracized character. This sturdy act of kindness sparks a useful domino impact inside the social circle. It encourages a welcoming surroundings wherein every body feels preferred and encouraged, and it efficaciously prevents bullying.

Building Coping Skills and Emotional Resilience

Coping capabilities are critical for minors to navigate lifestyles's worrying situations and maintain their emotional properly-being. Caregivers also can educate them essential tools for handling severa conditions with the resource of letting them apprehend and precise their feelings in suitable approaches.

Let's appearance extra cautiously at a few practical coping techniques: deep respiratory carrying activities, journaling, problem-fixing capabilities, and building a supportive surroundings.

A smooth but powerful technique for supporting kids in managing pressure and regaining internal calm is deep respiratory physical sports activities. Teaching them to take gradual, deep breaths after they experience beaten or afraid will supply them a device they may be capable of use anywhere and at any time. Assist your child to inhale deeply via their nostril, hold it for a 2nd, and then gently set free air via their lips. This technique starts offevolved the frame's rest response, this is particularly beneficial even as you're confused or annoying.

Imagine yourself in a situation in which your thoughts are racing and your coronary heart is pounding—deep respiration will come to the rescue! When a enormous test is developing, believe which you are a 9-twelve months-vintage and feeling disturbing. Well, you aren't through the use of yourself! We've all been there—loads of us. The proper information is that deep respiration is a clean but effective technique you can use to triumph over your nerves. If you enjoy demanding, don't forget getting cushty, final your eyes, and taking some slow, deep breaths. Take a deep breath in and lightly permit it out to allow the anxiety to melt away.

Journaling is every different excellent coping approach. Giving them a committed pocket book or mag allows them to freely precise their thoughts, feelings, and problems. They can explicit their feelings and benefit an facts of their anxieties thru journaling. Your teen want to be recommended to write approximately their research, demanding conditions, and successes. Reflecting on their mind and emotions might probably help youngsters amplify effective coping mechanisms and a more information in their emotions.

The significance of journaling as a device for emotional law for a young person underneath pressure from instructional and extracurricular commitments is highlighted within the following example. The toddler's mother and father have been aware about their growing anxiety and offered to present them a pocket e-book to assist them deal with their excessive feelings. The act of journaling come to be tough on the start, however after some time and continual attempt, it have grow to be second nature. The little one placed protection in the pocket book as an area to brazenly proportion every day critiques, desires, aspirations, and fears. Through this technique, they have been capable of launch their emotions and acquire insightful understanding approximately their issues. Through using a magazine, they have been able to higher recognize their feelings and understand stress-discount techniques, which over the years progressed their coping and emotional health.

Educating youngsters approximately trouble-fixing abilties is likewise a part of constructing resilience. Encourage them to divide hard responsibilities into small steps. For example, if your toddler is feeling beaten via a primary challenge, assist them create a to-do listing and prioritize chores. This method teaches youngsters a systematic technique to problem-fixing, which keeps them from feeling beaten via manner of the scale of the project to hand. They boom a feel of manipulate and achievement as they improvement with the aid of breaking matters down into smaller, greater possible steps.

In this subsequent situation, a ten-one year-vintage turned into supplied with a hard paintings assignment for a university competition. The younger individual considered the challenge to be too tough and did no longer understand wherein to start. Fortunately, having parental resource made matters less complicated because of the reality they were capable of divide the task into greater possible chunks. The intimidation of the teenager diminished while several steps have been identified, together with growing with mind, shopping for substances, and focusing on particular factors of the paintings. The methodical technique used to address each step stimulated and stimulated the younger character. Because of this, the pupil successfully completed the assignment and understood the fee of dividing massive duties into smaller, greater achievable chunks. This enjoy demonstrates the beneficial outcomes of such an method, allowing a more revel in of success and methodical problem-solving.

It is vital for caregivers to create a supportive and nurturing surroundings at domestic. Spending exceptional time together doing sports activities that encourage relaxation and amusing can greatly help kid's resilience. Plan sports sports for the complete own family, which includes board video video games, nature hikes, or creative pursuits like painting or cooking. These sports allow children to bond whilst furthermore relieving stress. They have a revel in of safety within the circle of relatives unit due to those shared reviews, know-how they have got a useful useful resource form on which to depend.

Encourage open conversation and energetic listening within the circle of relatives as well. Create a safe place in which your infant can specific their emotions with out annoying approximately being criticized. Let them comprehend which you understand their feelings and which you are to be had to assist. Actively be aware about their issues and memories on the identical time as demonstrating empathy and compassion. You set up get hold of as actual with and deepen your connection with your toddler through encouraging open conversation, it really is vital for his or her emotional nicely-being and resilience.

Due to her social obligations and homework, a thirteen-year-vintage female frequently felt overburdened. Her family started out preserving "own family take a look at-in" sessions due to this. Everyone inside the family took turns sharing the highs and lows in their days inside the route of these get-togethers. For the lady, taking part on this interest furnished a steady place to percentage her feelings and issues due to the fact she became conscious that her circle of relatives turned into looking and listening. She felt greater comfy and confident due to those test-ins. A more potent enjoy of belonging come to be additionally installed within the circle of relatives because of this hobby. In quit, the "family test-in" changed into introduced to help the female let loose her pent-up feelings and make more potent the own family dating.

Promoting a Growth Mindset and a Positive Outlook

The concept that talents may be developed via try and perseverance is referred to as a boom thoughts-set. Encouragement of a boom mind-set in youngsters can dramatically improve their resilience, permitting them to face obstacles with self guarantee and see screw ups as possibilities for improvement. In this phase, we're able to examine some realistic strategies to assist them extend a boom mind-set and a powerful attitude. We can permit them to create a resilient mindset that propels them to succeed by manner of reframing how we communicate approximately accomplishments and setbacks, setting realistic goals, and teaching thankfulness and exquisite questioning.

Reframing Achievements and Setbacks

It is crucial to reframe how we apprehend accomplishments and disappointments at the same time as promoting a developmental mind-set in college students. Instead of focusing in reality on outcomes, we should regulate our praise to apprehend their attempt, development, and perseverance. By doing this, we instill in them the experience that their efforts are valuable, no matter the immediate consequences.

Consider a little one who is struggling in school with a first rate challenge. Rather than focusing simply on their teachers, it's far essential to understand their endurance and effort in growing. Recognize the time they spend learning, getting assist, and taking detail actively of their education. This recognition will assist students internalize the idea that their skills aren't constant and that with persistent paintings, they could overcome troubles thru showcasing their self-control and perseverance.

When youngsters experience failure, it's far essential to train them to appearance it as a transitory stumbling block on their course to fulfillment. We help them increase a resilient mind-set by the use of using reframing setbacks as opportunities for improvement and gaining knowledge of. Remind them that setbacks are a everyday part of gaining knowledge of and that everyone encounters boundaries alongside the way to success. Encourage them to think about what they located from the setback and the way they may cope with the scenario in a awesome way next time.

We shift the emphasis from constant abilities to the way of increase and improvement by way of the usage of using stressing strive, improvement, and resilience. This shift in mindset teaches them that their well well well worth is measured now not best thru the effects they achieve however moreover by way of the usage of way of their willingness to paintings hard and persevere. It instills self guarantee and tenacity in children, motivating them to face worrying situations and strive for achievement.

Setting Realistic Goals

Cultivating a increase mindset consists of coaching youngsters the price of putting realistic goals and lowering huge goals down into smaller, greater ability milestones. This approach lets in kids experience improvement and accomplishment alongside the manner, encouraging their perception in their capabilities to take a look at and enlarge. Caregivers can offer advantageous reinforcement, urge children to persevere, and growth their self guarantee in handling destiny troubles through encouraging them to set low-cost dreams and praising every a hit try.

Think of a infant who is reading to enjoy a motorbike. Rather than expecting them to journey fantastically from the start, inspire them to set smaller goals that little by little boom their competencies and self warranty. These obligations ought to embody balancing for a few seconds, steerage easily, or pedaling independently for quick distances. They can enjoy concrete improvement and a sense of fulfillment by using the use of specializing in the ones practicable desires.

It is imperative for caregivers to famend even the smallest successes, irrespective of how trivial they'll appear. Recognize the kid's efforts and improvements at every degree. This confirmation strengthens their power of will and resiliency at the same time as encouraging a first rate outlook that welcomes learning and development. They examine that their efforts rely and that they will be able to overcoming limitations through being in an environment wherein even the tiniest accomplishments are stated and celebrated.

These little celebrations are effective motivators for kids. The encouraging comments they get enables them experience higher about themselves and motivates them to maintain going no matter the reality that subjects are tough. They moreover get a better revel in in their improvement and the movements important to carry out their last dreams by means of using breaking large goals down into extra possible steps. This readability gives them the energy to take fee in their training and cultivates a experience of competence and independence.

Setting less expensive objectives moreover lets in kids to enjoy small victories, which feeds their intrinsic motivation. Each a achievement strive serves as a foundation, advancing them and boosting their self-guarantee. They grow to be more open to taking over new traumatic situations once they see their private personal increase and development due to the truth they're extra awesome that they're capable of reap some element they placed their minds to with tough paintings and determination.

Nurturing Gratitude and Optimism

An vital element in selling resilience in youngsters is a fantastic attitude. We can also assist them in cultivating a resilient mentality via encouraging them to pay interest at the super additives in their lives and specific gratitude for even the little subjects. Establishing a own family gratitude exercising is one effective approach for cultivating thankfulness.

Think about enforcing a circle of relatives appreciation exercise into your every day regular, which encompass sharing gratitude on the dinner table or right earlier than bed. This easy hobby teaches minors to understand the splendid subjects in their each day lives and modifications their attitude. It nudges people to look beyond barriers and disappointments and appreciate the notable matters about their memories.

Participating in wonderful sports with children can help them increase resilience and a exquisite mind-set. Affirmation exercise is one such exercise. Encourage them to say matters which can be flattering about their abilties and capabilities to help them agree with in their very very own functionality. They ought to mention things like, "I am resilient and may recover from setbacks," or "I am capable of overcoming demanding situations." They accumulate a sturdy revel in of self and create an remarkable self-photo even as they may be regularly advised that they're capable.

These exercises help them reframe their recollections, which not first-rate promotes gratitude and optimism however also builds resilience. They are higher prepared to stand problem with the resource of emphasizing the positives and growing a exceptional attitude. They undertake a attitude that sees setbacks as possibilities for development and as transitory setbacks.

By organising self assure of their own abilities and generating a enjoy of empowerment, thankfulness, and superb wondering, they may be able to increase resilience. Additionally, it motivates humans to technique troubles with a solution-focused mindset and search for possibilities for gaining knowledge of and development.

We can actively interact within the ones sports activities as caregivers via emulating thankfulness and fantastic thinking. By operating in the direction of gratitude and affirmations ourselves, we are able to show children how important and useful those practices are. By encouraging appreciation and positivity, we construct resilient, upbeat students who're higher capable of with a piece of good fortune confront the demanding conditions of life.

Chapter 7: Parental And Teacher Involvement

To create a steady and supportive mastering environment, dad and mom and instructors need to be worried. The prevention of bullying and the encouragement of various characteristic-primarily based absolutely totally student behavior are two critical additives of this involvement. We can correctly fight this trouble by means of the usage of on foot with dad and mom, coaching educators about bullying and how to reply to it, and fostering open channels of communication among dad and mom, teachers, and children. This financial disaster examines the importance of those three elements and gives pointers and examples that could help students and their caregivers placed them into workout.

Collaborating with Parents to Address Bullying and Reinforce Positive Behaviors

Understanding the Importance of Parental Involvement

Parental have an effect on has a massive impact on how youngsters behave and develop socially. The significance of dad and mom in shaping their toddler's reviews, attitudes, and behaviors has been frequently emphasised with the beneficial aid of lecturers. They can also moreover furthermore take a look at virtues like empathy and a dislike of bullying from parents who're actively concerned in their lives as properly.

Regular discussions of feelings and war resolution serve as the cornerstones for developing requirements that deliver children the self notion to confront bullying. They revel in extra relaxed expressing themselves on the identical time as there may be an open speak approximately feelings and emotions. By talking approximately actual-existence conditions and promoting mindset-taking, mother and father can teach them to discover various feelings, understand their personal feelings, and bring together empathy for others. Parents can prevent bullying behavior through teaching minors about how their movements have an effect on different human beings and instilling in them a sense of duty and empathy.

Parents can recognition on warfare selection strategies at some point of the ones commands in addition to speaking about emotions. By training fundamental talents like hassle-solving, assertive conversation, and lively listening, mother and father offer their little ones with the abilities they want to solve disagreements amicably. They are much more likely to deal with disagreements correctly and assertively if they'll be taught the charge of respecting others' limits, speakme out for his or her very personal desires and thoughts in a courteous way, and seeking out collectively beneficial answers. This decreases the opportunity that they may interact in bullying or turn out to be its victims.

Parents can also serve as exquisite function fashions for their kids. Parental behavior has a robust effect on kids because of the truth they watch and select out up on it. Parents set an instance for his or her children to conform with with the useful aid of commonly demonstrating compassion, knowledge, and appreciate for others. The values that mother and father need to impart to their babies are strengthened even as those behaviors are exhibited via deeds of kindness, which includes lending a hand to a neighbor, volunteering, or being compassionate within the route of these in need. These behaviors are internalized through minors, who are consequently extra inclined to expose prosocial trends and face up to bullying.

Parental participation is a dynamic way that takes into consideration both the effectiveness of figure-infant interactions and express training. The presence of lively mother and father who really care approximately, be aware of, and assist their youngsters has a huge have an impact on on the kid's average nicely-being. Parents lay a solid foundation for emotional connection, bear in mind, and open communication via manner of taking an energetic position in their little one's lifestyles. As a surrender quit result of this connection, kids feel secure confiding of their dad and mom for recommendation and beneficial aid in difficult activities, along aspect bullying instances.

Building Partnerships: Engaging Parents in Bullying Prevention

It is critical to include mother and father inside the communication approximately bullying and lift their know-how of the trouble. Together, schools, instructors, and mother and father can also expand a collaborative technique that improves preventative and intervention efforts. Organizing decide assist agencies and net website hosting workshops and seminars are green methods to get mother and father worried in bullying prevention.

Workshops and seminars offer dad and mom useful probabilities to find out about figuring out and coping with bullying activities. These seminars, which may be planned via using educational institutions, community businesses, or faculties, offer mother and father with a dialogue board to find out about the various varieties of bullying, the caution signs to appearance out for, and green intervention measures. Workshops will also be used to inform dad and mom approximately the immediately and prolonged-time period results of bullying on children' nicely-being, stressing the need of performing fast. Parents who take part in the ones courses have a greater information of the techniques of bullying, allowing them to be extra proactive in spotting and handling bullying conditions.

In addition to seminars, growing discern help agencies can assist mother and father interact, percentage reports, and change strategies in a solid and galvanizing setting. These corporations supply dad and mom a dialogue board to speak about their troubles, get help, and offer you with practical answers for coping with bullying activities. Parents foster a sense of network and cooperation via replacing non-public opinions, effective interventions, and even their very personal troubles. Parents who may also moreover experience overburdened or uncertain approximately the way to govern bullying conditions can find out emotional help, validation, and useful advice on this collaborative placing. Parent assist organizations moreover supply parents the chance to analyze from each different's memories, fostering the development of a body of expertise that can be utilized in numerous situations.

Parent guide organizations provide benefits past virtually converting evaluations. They can act as a venue for inviting specific visitors, specialists, or experts in the region of bullying prevention to provide recommendation and facts. These humans also can offer sensible guidelines, proof-primarily based strategies, and information of the maximum present day trends inside the location of bullying prevention. Parents who have get entry to to these materials can increase their information and abilties in dealing with bullying sports in an green way. Parent guide corporations also can assist parents be part of and shape organizations, a very good manner to enhance the entire help device and forge a unified the the front in the direction of bullying.

Empowering Parents: Strategies for Addressing Bullying

In addressing and stopping bullying activities, parents are crucial. Parents require tools, course, and strategies that assist them pick out out and deal with bullying conditions with the intention to help their youngsters successfully.

By providing mother and father with the facts and direction they want to help their toddler, bullying occurrences can be identified and addressed. Pamphlets, internet internet web sites, and workshops that describe the numerous sorts of bullying and offer recommendation on intervention strategies can be made to be had via using colleges and community companies. These materials assist tell dad and mom of the telltale indicators of bullying, like behavioral modifications, injuries that cross undiagnosed, or social withdrawal. Parents can take early and effective movement to guard their youngsters via recognizing the ones caution signs and symptoms.

The functionality to speak successfully with their youngsters is a capability that mother and father also can observe. Parents can teach their children a manner to behave assertively and resist bullying by the usage of arming them with assertiveness and conflict choice abilities. Parents can feature-play severa scenarios to assist them advantage the self-guarantee and skills vital to express their emotions and set limitations in an aggressive way. These verbal exchange capabilities allow them to talk up for themselves and ask for assistance once they want it, promoting resilience and assertiveness.

Additionally, it is essential to foster prosocial and empathetic behaviors in the context of the own family. Beyond the have a take a look at room setting, dad and mom can actively promote a nice and inclusive environment. Parents can also moreover moreover help their kids keep near particular human beings's viewpoints and cultivate compassion through the usage of fostering empathy in them. They may additionally have discussions that emphasize the fee of treating people pretty and with empathy. They can speak approximately compassion, respect, and information. Parents can function function fashions with the useful useful resource of performing acts of kindness and inspiring their children to keep in thoughts the emotions and reviews of others.

Training Educators on Recognizing and Responding to Bullying Incidents

The Role of Educators in Bullying Prevention

Teachers are critical gamers inside the prevention and intervention of bullying situations because of the fact they have got a massive impact on college students' attitudes and behaviors. Teachers can set up effective social interactions and save you bullying through growing sturdy relationships with their college students which is probably built on mutual recognize and accept as true with.

One of the vital aspect responsibilities of teachers is to foster a way of life of understand, empathy, and appreciation in the check room. Teachers can set easy expectancies for conduct and feature position fashions for the ones beliefs thru their words and deeds. Teachers foster a climate in which bullying is tons much less likely to show up thru time and again stressing the cost of compassion, expertise, and reputation.

To efficaciously prevent and manipulate bullying, a supportive environment between instructors and college university college students is crucial. When confronted with bullying conditions, more youthful ones are more willing to are trying to find recommendation and help in the occasion that they experience a connection to their professors. Teachers can actively pay attention to college students' problems, widely recognized their opinions, and offer the right path and movement via encouraging open channels of conversation.

Through lots of techniques, teachers can actively contribute to growing a healthful study room environment. They can behavior collaborative analyzing wearing sports that sell teamwork and collaboration, permitting youngsters to broaden in empathy and shape healthy relationships with their friends. By introducing training that emphasize empathy, conflict decision, and problem-solving strategies into the curriculum, teachers can also encourage prosocial behavior. Teachers can equip students to resolve conflicts respectfully and nonviolently through way of explicitly education those capabilities.

In addition to bullying prevention projects, educators need to be looking for bullying situations and deal with them rapid. Teachers who are aware about the signs and symptoms and symptoms of bullying can spot while a child is being bullied or exhibiting bullying behavior. To save you bullying episodes from worsening and to shield the protection of all kids involved, a hard and fast off reaction is crucial.

To create entire anti-bullying rules and preventative programs, teachers can paintings collectively with precise university personnel individuals together with counselors and administrators. Teachers can beautify their know-how of the trouble and gather beneficial intervention techniques via using using taking detail in professional improvement sports activities activities which may be focused on bullying prevention. With the assist of this ongoing schooling, instructors can efficaciously deal with bullying occasions and installation a everyday mastering surroundings.

Building Educator Competence

In order to offer a welcoming and stable learning environment, educators need to benefit information of to understand the telltale signs and symptoms of bullying and to distinguish it from precise issues. Educators are better able to confront bullying activities and help each the victim and the bully while the desired understanding and skills are furnished to them. Opportunities for professional improvement are critical for supporting human beings preserve and amplify their abilities in this issue.

The first step in preventing bullying for educators is identifying its signs and symptoms. Teachers can observe the severa kinds of bullying, including cyberbullying and physical, verbal, social, and interpersonal bullying, through schooling packages. By being aware about the numerous styles of bullying, educators can spot capability times and act fast to interfere. They can studies to distinguish bullying from unique disagreements in order that the proper interventions may be made.

Bullying incidents can be significantly reduced by using the usage of the use of enforcing effective look at room manipulate techniques. Teachers can select up strategies for creating a welcoming surroundings within the observe room in which empathy, respect, and variety are valued. Teachers set the tone for appropriate behavior and foster a steady surroundings for all college students with the aid of laying out clean expectancies and tips. Professional improvement packages can supply teachers beneficial recommendation on the manner to govern lecture room dynamics, inspire wholesome peer relationships, and prevent bullying.

Giving educators get admission to to intervention strategies is important for coping with bullying occurrences as they arise. Training courses can show educators a way to react to allegations of bullying in a properly timed and appropriate way, ensuring the help of all events. Teachers can accumulate efficient communication strategies for handling the scenario with the affected university students and the sufferer's own family. In order to facilitate peace and inspire exceptional behavior change, they also can acquire schooling in restorative practices, struggle selection strategies, and mediation strategies.

Opportunities for ongoing professional improvement are crucial for boosting educators' capacity to deal with bullying. The prevention and remedy of bullying may be the concern of ordinary training periods, workshops, and seminars supplied by using the use of colleges. These expert development applications might also feature tourist audio system, trouble-count variety specialists, and chances for educator collaboration on studying and the change of pleasant practices. Educators can continuously enhance their abilties and modify to converting problems in managing bullying activities via way of keeping up with the most ultra-modern research and answers.

Educators can gain from peer mentoring and guide networks in the college network in addition to professional schooling. By fostering a collaborative environment wherein educators may additionally moreover proportion research, problems, and success recollections, we can create a high quality setting for lifelong gaining knowledge of. Peer statement packages or expert gaining knowledge of companies can resource facts sharing and offer comments and course to educators on their approaches to bullying prevention and intervention.

Chapter 8: Resources And Further Support

The combat in opposition to bullying need to interest on making colleges welcoming and consistent for all university college students Simply acknowledging the trouble won't be sufficient; we moreover need to offer people and agencies the machine they want to address and save you bullying. We can provide useful information and property to humans engaged in anti-bullying efforts thru recommending greater resources which includes books, internet web sites, and helpline connections.

Children may have a have a look at hundreds about bullying, empathy, and resilience through books. Age-appropriate books that have a take a look at those thoughts can provide insightful records and beneficial useful resource them in comprehending the effects of their alternatives greater absolutely. On the alternative hand, net web sites provide outcomes to be had facts and attractive assets that contain youngsters, dad and mom, and educators in the anti-bullying communicate. Online assets are adequate and consist of videos, guidelines, and processes that can be used to well turn out to be privy to bullying activities and deal with them.

For people impacted with the useful aid of bullying, helpline connections are crucial lifelines that provide quick useful resource and path. Help is continually reachable due to the guide and property supplied via countrywide and community helplines. These hotlines provide a consistent putting in which human beings can communicate about their evaluations, get steering, and get extra help. Making helplines honestly to be had and regarded ensures that people aren't struggling in silence.

Another critical trouble of supplying property and help is suggesting sports sports and sports activities to sell anti-bullying messages. Activities in the test room can display off empathy and recognize, encouraging students to do not forget numerous viewpoints and bring together vital social-emotional skills. They can discover their emotions and unfold reputation about bullying through many innovative forms, together with artwork and progressive expression. By concerning the network in anti-bullying sports activities like gatherings, workshops, and partnerships, the message is sent similarly and a experience of shared responsibility for addressing and stopping bullying is fostered.

The key to retaining anti-bullying tasks is to sell chronic conversation and assist for youngsters, dad and mom, and educators. By putting in safe locations via peer useful resource agencies, mentorship programs, and counseling services, it's far feasible for kids to get the path and assist they require. As parents can be geared up with expertise, strategies, and networks to successfully take care of bullying, their engagement is important to providing ongoing assist. Collaboration amongst educators and educator training improves colleges' capability to address and prevent bullying occasions.

Recognizing the fee of assets and additional assist will allow humans and groups to fight bullying on the the front strains. We can assemble a society wherein every toddler feels secure, professional, and valued through supplying extra belongings, recommending profitable activities, and provoking regular communique and guide.

Providing Additional Resources, Such as Books, Websites, and Helpline Contacts

Books:

Books have a extensive effect on children, giving them a window into the area and teaching them essential classes on pressing issues like bullying, empathy, and resilience. Age-appropriate books might also additionally effectively train youngsters about those issues via manner of the usage of the electricity of literature, assisting them in getting a higher draw near of the results in their alternatives and galvanizing empathy in them.

Books like "The Bully Blockers Club" with the aid of Teresa Bateman or "The Recess Queen" through using Alexis O'Neill may be excellent alternatives for them. In those novels, essential training like kindness, inclusion, and retaining off bullying are taught thru sympathetic characters and charming storytelling. They deliver to more youthful readers the belief that everybody is deserving of understand and that it's miles vital to address others with information and compassion.

Books that pass in addition into the complexities of bullying and empathy may be useful as youngsters broaden old. "Wonder" by using manner of the use of R.J. Palacio is one awesome example. This extraordinary-selling ebook explores the thoughts of empathy and popularity via telling the story of a more youthful toddler who struggles with social and educational troubles due to a facial difference. The novel gives an entire lot of viewpoints, enticing readers to assume themselves inside the characters' footwear and better apprehend the significance of their deeds and phrases.

They can find out feelings, get new views, and don't forget their very own conduct via analyzing novels which have realistic characters and situations. Reading can also moreover assist them extend their empathy, apprehend the impacts of bullying extra absolutely, and discover ways to address it. In a constant environment presented thru books, they will technique complex emotions, ask questions, and develop in empathy and admire for others.

Websites:

Websites are critical for imparting with out problem to be had statistics and bullying prevention techniques. Online structures make vital data without issues available via supplying significant assets for children, parents, and educators. Websites like StopBullying.Gov act as centralized centers and provide pretty some statistics on identifying, stopping, and managing bullying. These net websites provide statistics on numerous factors of bullying, which include its severa manifestations, caution signals, and intervention strategies, within the shape of articles, guides, and reality sheets. They additionally provide beneficial advice on the manner to assist dad and mom which is probably being bullied or witnessing bullying situations for mother and father and instructors.

The capability of on line structures to interact children via interactive elements is one in every of their strengths. Games, films, and interactive sporting activities are used on internet internet websites like PACER's Kids Against Bullying and Cartoon Network's Be a Buddy, Not a Bully to decorate anti-bullying instructions. Children discover it more terrific and relatable to examine bullying prevention manner to the ones exciting components. They can examine important talents approximately kindness, empathy, and conflict decision in a fun and interactive way via games and interactive storytelling. By looking films supplying relevant characters and cutting-edge-day sports activities, they may find out about the outcomes of their alternatives.

Additionally, the ones web web websites frequently embody resources mainly designed for numerous age businesses, making sure that the content material cloth fabric is pertinent and age-suitable. They deliver data in a way that is intelligible and relatable to college students of each age even as maintaining in thoughts their developmental degrees. This makes certain that kids can have interaction with the cloth at their non-public degree of statistics.

Helpline Contacts:

Helplines are vital equipment that provide activate beneficial aid and path to oldsters which are the dreams of bullying. Children, parents, and educators searching for help in handling the problems related to bullying can turn to national helpline connections much like the National Bullying Helpline or neighborhood helplines run thru businesses like STOMP Out Bullying.

These hotlines provide human beings with a strong setting wherein they'll percent their opinions, get steerage, and get get right of entry to to beneficial assets. These helplines are staffed by means of using manner of knowledgeable specialists or volunteers, ensuring that callers get keep of compassionate and ready care. The human beings walking the helplines are licensed to offer advice on dealing with bullying occasions, comprehending jail rights, and searching into ability intervention options.

It is vital to have helpline numbers to be had normally thinking about that this assures that help is best a cellphone call away. Promoting helpline contacts and spreading statistics about their availability can be extensively aided by the usage of schools, network centers, and anti-bullying organizations. These phone numbers may be made available just so humans can contact help once they maximum want it via posting them in faculty halls, on instructional materials, or on websites.

People can count on a kind and discreet environment whilst calling a hotline. Callers are invited to talk about their troubles and recollections for the reason that they will be heard without passing judgment. Depending on the caller's dreams, the hotline body of workers can provide emotional assist, beneficial recommendation, and get right of entry to to assets like counseling programs, guide corporations, or legal help.

Helplines are a exceptional resource for every bully patients and parents and teachers looking for advice on a way to assist humans who have been harmed. Parents can get recommendations on a manner to manipulate interactions with their youngsters, techniques for recording occurrences, and records at the way to engage with faculties. Teachers may additionally furthermore take a look at greater approximately a way to intervene effectively, foster a extraordinary university climate, and prevent bullying.

Chapter 9: Educating The Bully

Understanding the foundation causes of bullying conduct is important for coping with and stopping it. Bullying can be due to a selection of factors, which encompass non-public problems, a preference for energy and manage, and a loss of powerful coping mechanisms. Bullies hire this method to undertaking their very very own strength or cowl their non-public inadequacies. Knowing these items lets in one to approach bullies with empathy and a desire to assist them conquer their issues.

When thinking about the influences of a bully's surroundings, upbringing, and private evaluations, a fuller photo of their worldview is discovered. One's upbringing has a huge have an effect on on their perspectives and behavior. A bully's worldview would probably become a give up result of violent or negligent parenting, exposure to violence, or character bullying critiques. Their perception of electricity dynamics additionally can be stimulated through cultural factors like peer stress and media have an impact on. Recognizing the ones elements allows early motion, the supplying of help and path, and the advertising and marketing of pinnacle conduct to adjust their perspective.

It takes empathy and attitude-taking to steer bullies to alternate. Perspective-taking permits people to appearance topics from one-of-a-kind human beings's views, even as empathy is being aware of and feeling other humans's feelings. Bullies can understand the ache they motive their sufferers by using encouraging empathy and mind-set-taking, which might also inspire them to behave in a one of a kind manner and cope with others with appreciate and kindness. Fostering social interactions that decorate information is an essential a part of developing empathy, as is training bullies a manner to control their feelings.

To encourage trade, it's far crucial to approach bullies with empathy, compassion, and the possibility for personal growth. The basis for exchange is laid with the aid of figuring out the underlying causes of their behavior, thinking about the effect in their upbringing and prior stories, and stressing the importance of empathy and attitude-taking. Bullies can be persuaded to engage in healthy behaviors and given the belongings to gather wholesome relationships with the use of targeted interventions, assist structures, and educational programs. The reason of society is to create a extra compassionate and inclusive surroundings for truely all and sundry through addressing important issues and fostering empathy.

Empathy and Self-Reflection

Encouraging Bullies to Reflect on Their Actions and the Impact They Have on Others

In the subsequent instance, we come upon someone who has a information of bullying and is now centered on a scholar who wears glasses. However, after giving it a few intense concept, this character found out the importance of taking a second to take into account their actions and how they will have an effect on others. They started to recognize the viable pain their harsh conduct want to create thru thinking about the results in their words and deeds.

They found out empathy by means of the use of consciously setting themselves in their classmates' shoes through introspection. Through developing expertise of others' emotions, they had been capable of see how their dangerous feedback had made their classmate revel in worthless and self-acutely aware about sporting spectacles.

This student made the selection to magazine so you can growth extra self-reputation and empathy. They recorded their tales with bullying, their emotions, and the responses of the human beings that that they had focused on this diary. They were capable of face the results in their movements way to this exercise, which additionally promoted personal development.

They decided to regulate their behavior due to this profound perception and introspective journey. They truly apologized to their classmate and desired responsibility for his or her behavior. This demonstration of remorse and expertise resulted internal the arrival of a deeper and sincerer bond with the victim in their preceding bullying. It examined their improved capability for empathy and openness to considering the feelings of others, which ultimately had a superb impact on how they interacted with others.

Developing Empathy Skills Through Exercises and Discussions

Empathy is the capability to realize and enjoy the feelings of another person. This capacity can be picked up and superior over the years. Bullies need to pay attention on developing their empathy talents that lets in you to understand the consequences in their behavior and deal with others with love and understand. Empathy can be placed out greater effortlessly with the useful resource of manner of collaborating in sports activities and conversations that name for sufferers' mindset-taking. For example, one can be requested to compose a letter from the factor of view of a bullied individual, collectively with their feelings and thoughts. Through these sports activities, a deeper expertise of the struggling because of others and the importance of demonstrating empathy begins offevolved to emerge.

Attending programs that inspire empathy allows direct communication with the sufferers. Expressing remorse for one's behavior and listening to the sufferers' statements sooner or later of these instructions could probable sell empathy. Bonds can be fashioned thru the usage of empathizing with the sufferers' research, selling each recovery and personal development.

Fostering a Deeper Understanding of the Emotions and Experiences of Your Victims

Bullies typically overlook the emotional charge in their behavior to others. Fostering a better comprehension of the mind and studies of those impacted is essential if one desires to construct empathy. The stressful situations and lengthy-lasting emotional effects encountered through victims of bullying are highlighted via actual-existence tales or testimony from the ones who've skilled them. This attention might possibly result in honest remorse and a preference to make apologies.

It is probably instructive to check books or see movies that have a have a look at bullying and its affects. After such encounters, taking element in agency conversations allows one to analyze the characters' feelings. A better know-how of the significance of building a supportive surroundings for sufferers may be attained thru looking into the reasons, problems, and man or woman development of these humans.

Reading books or viewing movies about bullied folks who prevail could probably help one recognize the emotional repercussions of their behavior. Through introspection, one would in all likelihood extend empathy for the patients and are to be had to comprehend the need to foster a welcoming surroundings. This way may be aided through the usage of taking part in organization discussions which have a have a observe characters' development and resilience.

By selling reflected photograph on one's conduct and taking element in sports and conversations that sell empathy, the purpose is to growth popularity of the impacts of 1's conduct. The growth of empathy and self-consciousness may be facilitated thru fostering a more understanding of the thoughts and feelings of college college students who are laid low with bullying. Individuals may additionally moreover try and exchange their behavior and guide the improvement of society by doing this.

Addressing Misguided Beliefs and Attitudes

Challenging Distorted Thoughts and Beliefs That Contribute to Bullying Behavior

Bullies need to be confronted with their distorted perceptions and ideals that allows you to be pushed to alter their behavior. Bullies may additionally additionally have mind that help their movements, supporting them to rationalize their conduct. However, it's far important to understand that the ones thoughts often relaxation on defective right judgment and might appreciably injure different people.

For the transformation method to get began, growing critical thinking and thinking skills is important. This includes evaluating one's personal beliefs and thoughts even as taking into consideration numerous viewpoints. Individuals can discover ways to recognize misconceptions of their wondering and recognize the unfavourable effects of their behavior via taking part in sports activities that display screen them to numerous bullying situations, in addition to by means of the use of manner of having dialogues with others.

Participating in group sports activities activities that have a have a look at traditional bullying situations offers the threat to have open discussions approximately and debate the motivations at the back of the characters' moves.

Through this manner, people can also moreover venture their preconceived notions and cope with their non-public prejudices that underpin their bullying conduct.

Promoting Critical Thinking and Questioning Harmful Stereotypes

People can hotel to bullying due to destructive preconceptions that advocated their conduct. It is essential to actively have interaction in important thinking and deal with these preconceptions if one wants to have an open-minded outlook. Stereotypes restrict our potential for facts others and may cause unfair judgments and movements.

Exposure to reminiscences and media with characters that question the ones assumptions is important for overcoming volatile prejudices. By mastering about successful humans in professions which might be normally assigned to human beings of numerous genders, nationalities, or origins, preconceptions can be stressed and perspectives may be broadened.

Think about the following instance, even as a beyond bully made fun of Carlos for having a passion for dance. They located that ballet is a hard and cherished art shape via conversations that challenged gender stereotypes. They found out that it modified into better to apprehend Carlos' zeal than to belittle it. They commenced going to Carlos' ballet performances after seeing his strength of mind to show their assist. This tale serves as an instance of the transformational electricity of vital thinking and confronting bad stereotypes.

Introducing Alternative Perspectives and Promoting Tolerance and Acceptance

One want to actively inspire tolerance and recognition even as listening to many elements of view at the manner to exchange a bully's thoughts-set. Learning about one-of-a-kind cultures, religions, and identities helps expand one's attitude on the sector and fosters empathy and appreciate for awesome people.

Whenever possible, capture the possibility to have a examine from humans with unique backgrounds. Inquiries approximately human beings's cultures, customs, and evaluations may be made during interactive durations, which promotes extra information. These durations can take diverse paperwork, which incorporates workshops, institution discussions, seminars, indicates, or perhaps casual conversations.

It is a great deal less complex to collaborate on modern-day duties with human beings from numerous backgrounds while you're taking element in programs that sell cultural interchange. The importance of variety is highlighted, and recognition of it's miles facilitated through such interactions.

Participating in range tasks and ethnic celebrations gives get proper of access to to active debates and one of a kind sports that display human beings to severa elements of view. Through this interplay, one may additionally venture their private prejudices and advantage knowledge from others, fostering a honest appreciation for variety.

People can go through personal boom and transition a protracted manner from a bully thoughts-set by means of using hard wrong assumptions, fostering skepticism, and accepting exchange critiques. By assignment such sports sports, one could become greater accepting and tolerant of others, confront negative prejudices, and become more aware of their very own thinking limits.

A extra inviting and compassionate surroundings for all sports is facilitated via forceful motion taken to deal with the roots of bullying conduct.

Building Social Skills and Positive Relationships

Educating People in Appropriate Conflict Resolution and Communication Methods

Knowing the manner to speak efficiently and resolve conflicts is critical for folks who engage in bullying conduct. One can also beautify verbal exchange and clear up conflicts without the usage of bullying strategies through honing those competencies. To encourage the development of those capabilities, workshops and unique sports activities activities that pressure assertiveness, assertiveness education, and non-violent problem-solving are furnished.

Interactive function-playing intervals can assist to expand communication abilties. Participants in those workshops get the risk to play quite a few roles, which include victim, bully, and mediator. People might also discover about diverse elements of view and the results of their conversation fashion thru this hobby.

It's critical to pay interest on the same time as others are talking and to explicit one's very very own opinions with the aid of the use of "I" statements. Finding answers that artwork for all elements is likewise critical. These capabilities permit for progressed communication and the improvement of stronger bonds among humans. It is vital for caregivers and educators to assist people accumulate those critical capabilities.

Encouraging Positive Peer Interactions and Fostering Healthy Friendships

Through constructive interactions with friends, bullying conduct may be appreciably altered. Building a sturdy community of connections is possible while taking detail in cooperative sports activities like organization sports activities, organization responsibilities, or volunteer artwork. As they cooperate and show empathy for each different, this encourages the growth of collaboration, cooperation, and teamwork amongst classmates.

Take into account a person who has a records of bullying behavior. This individual made the choice to join the university's volunteer software, wherein they made buddies with humans from all backgrounds who all favored to have a incredible have an effect on thru volunteering. With the assist of their newfound connections, they were able to increase for my part and get over their pre-current bullying tendencies.

An surroundings this is supportive of personal increase may be created via promoting healthful relationships and taking detail in sports activities that encourage terrific peer interactions.

Promoting Respect for Boundaries and the Rights of Others

It's vital to apprehend and well known the rights and barriers of others which will have healthy relationships. It is vital to recognize that everyone has bodily and emotional barriers that ought to be taken under consideration. Conversations on personal boundaries and consent can be navigated with the help of caregivers and educators. They region emphasis on how vital it's far to widely recognized and recognize these obstacles.

Pupils can participate in interactive situations to higher recognize personal limitations and consent. These fictitious eventualities offer a stable environment for candid discussions on consent, constructing an understanding of the rate of getting consent in an entire lot of occasions. Everyone wishes to be handled with understand and decency, and this desires to be emphasized.

Chapter 10: Signs That Your Child Is Being Bullied

As a decide, it's far vital to be aware about the signs and symptoms that your little one may be experiencing bullying at college. Bullying may additionally have sizeable affects on a little one's physical and emotional fitness, similarly to their educational typical overall performance. In this chapter, we will find out the signs that your baby may be experiencing bullying at school and provide recommendation on a way to address this trouble.

Behavioral Changes in Your Child

One of the most common signs and symptoms and symptoms that a little one is being bullied at university is a trade in their behavior. Your little one may additionally end up extra withdrawn, traumatic, or depressed than ordinary. They can also moreover turn out to be greater irritable, without problem agitated, or angry. Other behavioral adjustments to take a look at out for encompass:

Avoidance of school or social sports activities activities: Your infant might also additionally furthermore try to avoid going to highschool or taking detail in sports they used to enjoy.

Changes in consuming and sleeping behavior: Your infant may additionally start to enjoy adjustments of their ingesting or sleeping behavior. They can also start to devour less, shed pounds, or have trouble sleeping.

Lack of hobby in faculty or sports: Your toddler may moreover come to be disinterested in school and their not unusual sports. They also can begin to lose motivation, and their grades also can begin to suffer.

Physical Signs of Bullying

Physical signs and symptoms and signs and symptoms of bullying can variety counting on the sort and severity of the bullying. However, there are some not unusual bodily signs and symptoms and signs and symptoms to appearance out for, along with:

Unexplained accidents: Your little one can also have bruises, cuts, or scratches that they cannot supply an motive for.

Changes in urge for meals or sleep styles: Your little one may additionally additionally experience changes of their urge for meals or sleep styles because of the pressure of the bullying.

Stomachaches and headaches: Your little one may experience stomachaches or headaches that cannot be attributed to each other motive.

Changes in Your Child's Academic Performance

Bullying also can have a big impact on a toddler's academic performance. If your baby is being bullied, you may word adjustments in their grades, along aspect a surprising drop in widespread overall performance. Other academic modifications to look at out for encompass:

Lack of interest in college: Your infant may become disinterested in school and their ordinary sports. They can also begin to lose motivation, and their grades may additionally additionally additionally begin to undergo.

Difficulty concentrating: Your baby may additionally additionally moreover have problem targeting their schoolwork due to the stress and anxiety of the bullying.

Increased absenteeism: Your toddler can also start to miss greater college than preferred due to the pressure of the bullying.

What to Do If You Suspect Your Child is Being Bullied

If you believe you studied that your infant is being bullied, it is vital to take action proper away. Here are some steps you can take:

Talk on your child. Start through speaking on your little one about what is taking location. Let them apprehend that you are there to useful resource them and that you want to help.

Contact the school: Contact your baby's faculty to tell them of the state of affairs. Ask to speak with a teacher, counselor, or administrator who can assist.

Encourage your infant to talk up. Encourage your infant to talk up in the event that they witness bullying conduct. Let them recognize that it's miles good enough to ask for help.

Provide emotional useful resource. Provide emotional help for your infant. Let them understand which you love and help them no matter what.

Being aware of the symptoms that your infant is being bullied at faculty is critical. Behavioral modifications, bodily symptoms, and adjustments in instructional performance can all be indicators of bullying. If you located that your infant is being bullied, it's miles critical to do so right away through speaking in your toddler, contacting the college, encouraging your infant to speak up, and offering emotional help.

Strategies to Support Your Child Who is Being Bullied at School

Bullying is a critical issue that impacts many youngsters, specifically the ones in school. It have to have a devastating effect on a toddler's arrogance and mental fitness, in addition to their ability to recognition in magnificence and experience faculty. As a discern, it is critical to apprehend the signs and symptoms and signs of bullying and take steps to help your infant. This chapter will offer techniques to beneficial useful resource your toddler who is being bullied at faculty, together with developing an open and supportive environment, the usage of powerful conversation strategies to assist your infant open up about the bullying, and supporting your little one construct resilience and coping mechanisms.

Creating an Open and Supportive Environment for Your Child

Creating a solid and supportive environment is important in terms of helping your toddler who is being bullied. It is important to make certain your little one is aware of that they could come to you for assist and help while they may be going via a difficult situation. Make sure to express your unconditional love and assist for your little one and allow them to realize that you are there for them. It is likewise vital to set smooth barriers and expectations in your toddler's conduct.

Make excessive excellent to have a 0-tolerance coverage for bullying and supply an reason of why it is vital to address others with understand.

Effective Communication Strategies to Help Your Child Open Up About Bullying

As a determine, it may be tough to apprehend at the same time as your toddler is being bullied. It is crucial to be aware of the symptoms of bullying and to take note of what your toddler is announcing and the way they are feeling. If you note any changes for your little one's behavior or mind-set, it is critical to speak to them about it. When speaking in your infant, it's far important to be affected character, information, and non-judgmental. Ask open-ended questions, which incorporates "How do you feel at the same time as a person makes amusing of you?" or "What do you decided we are capable of do to make subjects higher?". It is likewise vital to pay attention for your infant's solutions and validate their emotions.

Helping Your Child Build Resilience and Coping Mechanisms

It is important to help your toddler assemble resilience and coping mechanisms to address bullying. Encourage your baby to talk to depended on adults, together with teachers or faculty counselors. It is likewise essential to assist your toddler increase healthful coping mechanisms, in conjunction with exercise, journaling, or speakme to pals. Encourage your infant to upward push up for themselves while they are being bullied. Remind them that it is ok to be assertive and to set smooth boundaries with folks who are bullying them. Conclusion Bullying is a severe trouble that influences many children, and it could have a devastating impact on a infant's self-esteem and intellectual health. As a decide, it's far vital to apprehend the symptoms and signs and symptoms and signs and symptoms of bullying and take steps to assist your infant. This financial spoil has supplied techniques to help your infant who's being bullied at university, inclusive of creating an open and supportive surroundings, the usage of effective conversation strategies to help your toddler open up about the bullying, and supporting your little one build resilience and coping mechanisms.

Chapter 11: How To Work With Schools To Address School Bullying

The hassle of college bullying has been a primary hassle for decades, affecting loads of youngsters and teens. It is anticipated that one in 4 youngsters can be the victim of bullying in some unspecified time inside the destiny at some point of their faculty years. As mother and father, it's miles our duty to understand our rights and duties and to paintings collaboratively with teachers and administrators to ensure that our children are steady and constant within the faculty surroundings. In this financial disaster, we will communicate the way to art work with faculties to deal with bullying, in conjunction with records our rights and responsibilities as mother and father, taking element with teachers and administrators to cope with bullying, and advocating for our little one and developing a direction of motion.

Understanding Your Rights and Responsibilities as a Parent

As a discern, you have got were given the proper to be concerned to your infant's education and to be aware about the guidelines and strategies in place at their school. It is essential to apprehend your rights and obligations on the manner to efficaciously paintings with the university to cope with bullying. You have the proper to

Be knowledgeable of the manner the university deals with bullying.

Be worried in any selections regarding how the college deals with bullying.

Be notified in case your toddler is concerned in a bullying situation.

Be given the possibility to talk approximately any issues with university workforce.

Be involved in any disciplinary or useful resource measures performed with the aid of way of the college.

You additionally have the obligation to

Ensure that your little one is acquainted with the college's guidelines concerning bullying.

Encourage your toddler to file any incidents of bullying.

Follow thru with any disciplinary or assist measures implemented with the resource of the college.

Remain involved and keep verbal exchange open with college group of workers.

Collaborating with Teachers and Administrators to Address Bullying

It is vital to collaborate with teachers and directors on the way to correctly address the hassle of bullying. Here are a few hints for running with university personnel to deal with bullying:

Make certain to keep open verbal exchange with the college.

Ask questions and be inclined to pay attention to their perspectives.

Share any relevant data and research on bullying.

Work together to extend a route of motion to cope with bullying.

Advocating for Your Child and Creating a Plan of Action

Once you have got collaborated with school frame of people to boom a course of movement, it's miles important to make certain that your infant is protected and that their wishes are being met. Here are a few tips for advocating in your toddler and developing a course of motion:

Make sure your toddler knows their rights and is aware about a way to record any incidents of bullying.

Work with the school to create a stable surroundings to your infant.

Develop a path of movement that addresses the man or woman dreams of your toddler.

Make certain that your little one is covered in any disciplinary or guide measures carried out via using way of the college.

In give up, bullying is a critical problem that influences loads of kids each twelve months. As dad and mom, it's miles our obligation to apprehend our rights and duties and to paintings collaboratively with instructors and directors to make sure that our youngsters are stable and consistent inside the university environment. By information our rights and duties, taking part with university team of workers, and advocating for our youngsters, we are able to create a stable and supportive environment so that it will help them reap success.

Cyberbullying: What Parents Need to Know

As generation keeps to strengthen, so does the superiority of cyberbullying. As a determine, it's miles critical to understand what cyberbullying is, the manner it influences your infant, and what techniques you could use to protect them. In this bankruptcy, we are able to explore those topics massive, imparting valuable insights and actionable advice that will help you keep your child steady within the digital worldwide.

What is cyberbullying?

Cyberbullying is using technology to hassle, intimidate, or threaten a few extraordinary character. This can take many forms, along with sending hurtful messages, spreading rumors, posting embarrassing photos or movies, or growing faux profiles to impersonate a person else. Cyberbullying can get up on social media systems, thru textual content messages, emails, or specific digital channels.

One of the maximum insidious elements of cyberbullying is that it could be difficult to locate. Children can be reluctant to talk about their critiques or won't even apprehend they're being bullied. It is crucial for dad and mom to live vigilant and be aware about the warning signs and symptoms of cyberbullying, along with changes in conduct, withdrawal from social activities, or reluctance to use their mobile phone or laptop.

The Impact of Cyberbullying on Children

The results of cyberbullying may be devastating for kids. Victims may additionally experience despair, anxiety, and occasional shallowness. They may also warfare with instructional common ordinary performance or maybe keep in mind self-harm or suicide. The anonymity and distance provided by way of way of virtual communication ought to make the effect of cyberbullying even greater immoderate, as youngsters can also revel in like there is no escape from their tormentors.

As a determine, it's far essential to take cyberbullying seriously and to help your toddler if they're experiencing it. Make powerful your little one is aware of that they may be capable of come to you for help and that you can take their concerns considerably. Encourage your infant to speak to a trainer, counselor, or different depended on character if they're being bullied. It is likewise essential to show your toddler's virtual interest and be privy to the structures they may be the use of.

Strategies to Protect Your Child from Cyberbullying

There are numerous techniques you can use to protect your toddler from cyberbullying. The first step is to speak on your child about net safety and the importance of being careful on line. Encourage your infant to count on considerably approximately the information they percentage and the people they speak with on line. Make positive they apprehend no longer to percentage non-public data or engage with strangers.

It is also critical to set clean suggestions and suggestions for your little one's net use. Establish regulations round the amount of time your toddler can spend on-line and what they could and can't do online. Make sure your toddler is aware of that you may be tracking their interest and that there might be results in the event that they violate your tips.

Another approach is to encourage your toddler to take a harm from generation. Encourage them to take part in activities that don't involve screens, which incorporates analyzing, gambling outside, or spending time with pals and circle of relatives. This can help your toddler expand a greater in shape dating with technology and reduce the threat of cyberbullying.

If your baby is experiencing cyberbullying, it's miles crucial to take action. Report the bullying to the platform or internet website wherein it is occurring, and endure in mind contacting law enforcement if the bullying is excessive or threatening. Work together together with your little one's university to increase a plan to deal with the bullying and guide your little one.

Chapter 12: The Role Of Mental Health

Bullying may additionally moreover have a profound emotional impact on children, frequently vital to intellectual fitness annoying situations which includes anxiety, melancholy, and publish-stressful stress infection (PTSD). In order to efficaciously deal with bullying, it's far essential to apprehend the emotional impact it may have on your little one and to locate the right intellectual health useful resource for them. In this economic disaster, we will find out the ones subjects large, providing treasured insights and actionable advice that will help you help your toddler's highbrow fitness inside the face of bullying.

Understanding the Emotional Impact of Bullying on Your Child

Bullying ought to have loads of emotional affects to your child, relying on their person temperament and the specific state of affairs. Some not unusual emotional responses to bullying embody fear, tension, disappointment, anger, and disgrace. These feelings may be immoderate and overwhelming, and might interfere in conjunction with your child's functionality to recognition on their instructional art work, hold relationships with buddies, and enjoy normal sports.

It is critical to concentrate to your infant and validate their emotions. Let them comprehend that what they're experiencing is real and which you are there to useful useful resource them. Help them to choose out and precise their emotions in healthful methods, including via journaling, drawing, or speakme with a relied on character.

Finding the Right Mental Health Support for Your Child

When it involves locating intellectual fitness help for your little one, there are numerous options to recollect. School counselors may be a valuable useful resource for helping your toddler navigate the emotional effect of bullying. They can offer a steady location for your toddler to speak approximately their emotions, offer coping strategies, and be part of your family with extra resources.

In addition to high school counselors, you can need to recall seeking out assist from a intellectual health expert, together with a therapist or psychologist. These experts are knowledgeable to assist youngsters approach their emotions and expand wholesome coping strategies. They also can offer you with steerage on a manner to incredible help your toddler at domestic.

It is vital to find out a highbrow fitness expert who focuses on operating with youngsters and has revel in with bullying-related troubles. Ask for hints from trusted friends, family participants, or your toddler's university counselor. You also can seek on-line for local vendors and have a look at evaluations from distinctive dad and mom.

Incorporating Mental Health Strategies into Your Child's Daily Routine

In addition to looking for outdoor assist, there are various intellectual health strategies that you could incorporate into your toddler's each day normal to assist them address the emotional impact of bullying. These techniques encompass:

Encouraging physical interest: Regular workout can assist to reduce stress and anxiety, and can also beautify temper and arrogance. Encourage your toddler to participate in sports sports or distinct bodily sports activities they enjoy.

Practicing mindfulness: Mindfulness practices, together with deep breathing and meditation, can help your toddler to live calm and targeted in the face of bullying. Consider downloading a mindfulness app or guiding your baby through a brief meditation each day.

Fostering social connections: Encourage your little one to maintain effective relationships with friends and to are in search of for out supportive friends. Help them to become aware about remarkable social sports activities they revel in, consisting of golf equipment or pastimes, and inspire them to take part frequently.

Modeling healthy coping techniques: Children studies via example, so it is essential to model wholesome coping strategies on your infant. Practice stress-reducing strategies, which embody deep respiration or yoga, in the the the front of your infant and talk to them approximately how those techniques assist you enjoy higher.

Bullying can have a profound emotional effect on youngsters, and it is critical to take steps to deal with the mental health annoying conditions that may rise up. By records the emotional impact of bullying on your infant, finding the proper intellectual fitness guide, and incorporating highbrow fitness strategies into your child's every day recurring, you can help your infant increase the skills and resilience they need to address bullying and thrive in all areas in their lifestyles.

Building Resilient and Confident Children

As mother and father, all of us want to elevate satisfied and assured kids who can cope with lifestyles's united statesand downs with grace and resilience. Building a infant's self-esteem and self guarantee takes effort and time, but it is nicely well well worth it. Here are some strategies for enhancing your infant's conceitedness, encouraging great social connections and activities, and supporting them increase resilience and confidence.

Strategies for Boosting Your Child's Self-Esteem

Self-esteem is the muse of self notion, so it is vital to assist your child increase a amazing self-image. Here are some processes to boost your toddler's arrogance:

Praise your toddler's efforts and accomplishments, not without a doubt their successes. This will help them revel in glad with their difficult art work, no matter the truth that they do no longer always win or get pinnacle marks.

Encourage your child to try new matters and take dangers. This will help them increase a sense of mastery and accomplishment, with a view to improve their self warranty.

Help your toddler perceive their strengths and capabilities. Focus on what they're right at, and inspire them to growth those talents further.

Provide opportunities on your toddler to make contributions to the own family or network. This will assist them sense valued and crucial.

Encouraging Positive Social Connections and Activities

Social connections and activities can assist your little one construct a revel in of belonging and increase their social skills. Here are a few methods to inspire exceptional social connections and sports activities:

Encourage your little one to join clubs, sports activities sports organizations, or awesome groups that hobby them. This will assist them make new friends and develop their social talents.

Plan ordinary playdates with extraordinary youngsters their age. This will offer them a chance to exercise socializing in a secure and supportive environment.

Help your toddler increase empathy and kindness via modeling the ones traits yourself and provoking them to show kindness to others.

Helping Your Child Develop Resilience and Confidence

Resilience is the capability to get better from setbacks and disturbing conditions, that is an critical capability for fulfillment in life. Here are a few strategies to help your little one expand resilience and self notion:

Encourage your little one to tackle worrying situations and setbacks as analyzing possibilities. Help them select out what they'll be able to analyze from the enjoy and the way they're able to use that statistics in the destiny.

Help your little one increase trouble-solving abilties by encouraging them to brainstorm answers to problems they come upon. This will help them enjoy empowered and confident of their capability to deal with demanding situations.

Teach your baby healthful coping strategies for pressure and anxiety, which includes deep respiratory or mindfulness bodily sports. This will help them revel in greater on top of factors in their feelings and better capable of control pressure.

Building resilient and confident children takes effort and time, however it's far worth it. By boosting your little one's vanity, encouraging effective social connections and sports activities, and supporting them increase resilience and self warranty, you could provide them the gear they need to attain lifestyles. Remember to model these dispositions yourself and be affected character and supportive as your toddler develops these capabilities.

Chapter 13: Legal Considerations

Bullying is a pervasive hassle in masses of colleges, and it is able to have devastating results at the highbrow and emotional fitness of kids. As a determine, it's far critical to apprehend the jail framework surrounding college bullying and your rights and options as a parent to guard your toddler.

Understanding the Legal Framework Surrounding School Bullying

Most states have felony pointers in place to cope with university bullying. These laws outline bullying as intentional and repeated damage, collectively with physical, verbal, or emotional abuse. They moreover set up tactics for reporting and investigating bullying incidents, further to results for college college students who've interaction in bullying behavior.

Additionally, faculties need to conform with federal legal guidelines, along with Title IX and Section 504 of the Rehabilitation Act, which shield university college college students from discrimination primarily based on their gender, race, disability, or exclusive elements. These laws require colleges to take steps to save you and cope with bullying and harassment and provide remedies for college kids who have been harmed.

Your Rights and Options as a Parent

As a figure, you have were given have been given the right to endorse on your toddler and ensure that their rights are included. If your infant has been bullied, there are numerous steps you may take to address the problem:

Report the bullying to highschool officials: If you emerge as aware about bullying, it's far critical to report it to high school officers. Schools are required to research and take suitable movement to cope with the bullying.

Keep statistics: Keep a record of all incidents of bullying, which encompass the date, time, region, and names of any witnesses. This information may be useful in case you want to make a complaint to the university or take jail motion.

Consult with an criminal expert: If the university does no longer take suitable motion to address the bullying or in case your infant has been seriously harmed, you can want to speak about with an legal expert who focuses on education regulation. They will will let you apprehend your criminal alternatives and take steps to guard your toddler.

Working with Legal Professionals to Address School Bullying

If you decide to work with an felony expert, they allow you to take several steps to cope with faculty bullying, which includes:

Filing a complaint with the school: Your legal professional let you file a proper complaint with the university, so you can motive an investigation into the bullying incident.

Pursuing jail movement: If the faculty does not take appropriate movement to cope with the bullying, your lawyer allow you to pursue criminal movement. This may additionally furthermore encompass submitting a lawsuit closer to the college or the scholar who engaged within the bullying behavior.

Advocating on your baby: Your attorney also can endorse on your toddler inside the course of the process, making sure that their rights are covered and that they get maintain of appropriate guide and lodges.

As a discern, it is vital to understand the jail framework surrounding college bullying and your rights and alternatives to shield your toddler. If your toddler has been bullied, take steps to document the bullying, maintain records, and discuss with an legal professional if vital. Working with criminal experts let you take powerful movement to cope with college bullying and defend your baby's rights.

When to Seek Professional Help

As a determine, it is able to be tough to recognize whilst your toddler is suffering with intellectual fitness problems that require professional help. Recognizing the signs and symptoms and taking movement early could make a large difference in your little one's well-being and fashionable fulfillment in life. In this monetary destroy, we're capable of discover the significance of recognizing at the same time as your infant dreams expert help, finding the proper intellectual health expert in your toddler, and incorporating expert help into your infant's direction of motion.

Recognizing When Your Child Needs Professional Help

It isn't always normally easy to recognize whilst your toddler wishes professional assist. Some signs and symptoms and signs and signs to examine out for encompass a considerable decline in instructional ordinary overall performance, adjustments in dozing or consuming conduct, withdrawal from social activities, stepped forward irritability or mood swings, and a lack of interest in topics they used to experience. If you be conscious any of those signs and symptoms, it's miles critical to do so and are trying to find expert help in your toddler.

Finding the Right Mental Health Professional for Your Child

There are many outstanding sorts of intellectual health specialists, and locating the right one for your infant is vital. A right vicinity to begin is with the useful resource of talking to your toddler's pediatrician or university counselor, who can advocate specialists in your region. You can also are trying to find online or ask for suggestions from pals or family contributors.

When selecting a intellectual health expert in your toddler, it is critical to don't forget their qualifications and experience, further to their method to treatment. Some youngsters may additionally reply higher to sure forms of therapy or counseling, so it's miles essential to discover a expert who can offer the proper sort of treatment to your child's specific needs.

Incorporating Professional Help into Your Child's Plan of Action

Once you've got were given placed the proper highbrow fitness expert in your little one, it's miles crucial to consist of their assist into your toddler's course of movement. This also can include everyday treatment durations, treatment, or a combination of every. It is essential to be supportive of your infant and to paintings closely with their intellectual health expert to make certain that they are receiving the fine feasible care.

In addition to expert help, it's also essential to incorporate self-care strategies into your infant's every day recurring. Encourage your little one to interact in sports they enjoy, get enough relaxation, devour a wholesome weight loss program, and spend time with friends and circle of relatives. These sports activities can help to enhance your child's normal well-being and resource their highbrow health.